Scott of the Antarctic

Also by Michael De-la-Noy

Elgar: The Man
Denton Welch: The Making of a Writer
The Honours System
Acting as Friends: The Story of the Samaritans
Eddy: The Life of Edward Sackville-West
Michael Ramsey: A Portrait
Windsor Castle: Past and Present
Exploring Oxford
The Church of England: A Portrait
The Queen Behind the Throne
The King Who Never Was: The Story of Frederick, Prince of Wales
Mervyn Stockwood: A Lonely Life

EDITED BY MICHAEL DE-LA-NOY

The Journals of Denton Welch
The Collected Short Writings of Denton Welch

Pocket BIOGRAPHIES

Scott of the Antarctic

MICHAEL DE-LA-NOY

SUTTON PUBLISHING

First published in 1997 by
Sutton Publishing Limited · Phoenix Mill
Thrupp · Stroud · Gloucestershire · GL5 2BU

British Library Cataloguing in Publication Data

A catalogue record for this book is available from the British
Library

ISBN 0-7509-1512-9

Typeset in 12/16 pt Perpetua.
Typesetting and origination by
Sutton Publishing Limited.
Printed in Great Britain by
The Guernsey Press Company Limited,
Guernsey, Channel Islands.

For

Marion and Bryan Breed

'Truth and right and justice were [Scott's] gods, and these did not come with any religious sense. They were something within himself. He led a decent human life because he was a decent human being.'

Louis Bernacchi, a physicist who accompanied
Captain Scott on his first Antarctic expedition,
The Saga of the 'Discovery' (Blackie & Sons, 1938)

'Victory awaits those who have everything in order – people call that luck. Defeat is certain for those who have forgotten to take the necessary precautions in time – that is called bad luck.'

Roald Amundsen, *My Life as an Explorer*
(Doubleday, Page & Co, 1927)

'With the sole exception of the death of Nelson in the hour of victory there has been nothing so dramatic.'

The journalist Hannen Swaffer, in conversation.

CONTENTS

ACKNOWLEDGEMENTS

For their valuable help I am greatly indebted to the following: Miss Beryl Bainbridge; Dr H.W. Dickinson of the Britannia Royal Naval College, Dartmouth; Miss Karen Gee of the Royal Geographical Society; the Headmistress of Stubbington House School, Ascot; Miss Emma Lodge, deputy librarian at the Royal Naval College, Greenwich; Lt Col Anthony Mather, secretary of the Central Chancery of the Orders of Knighthood; Canon Michael Moore, chaplain of the Chapel Royal, Hampton Court Palace; and Miss Shirley Sawtell of the Scott Polar Research Institute, Cambridge.

For biographical information about some of the members of Scott's Antarctic expeditions I have made liberal use of material to be found in *Scott of the Antarctic* (1977) by Elspeth Huxley, one of the best written and most comprehensive full-length studies of Scott yet attempted. For a more critical view of Scott I have taken into account a hard-hitting reappraisal of his character and conduct, *Scott and Amundsen* (1979), by Roland Huntford.

Michael De-la-Noy
Hove, 1997

CHRONOLOGY

6 June 1868	Born Devonport
1880?	Educated Stubbington House School, Fareham
15 July 1881	Enters HMS *Britannia*
24 July 1883	Joins HMS *Boadicea*
14 Aug. 1883	Becomes Midshipman
19 Sept. 1885	Joins HMS *Monarch*
1 Nov. 1886	Joins HMS *Rover*
1887	Acting Sub-Lieutenant
	Attends Royal Naval College, Greenwich
1888	Joins HMS *Amphion*
14 Aug. 1889	Lieutenant
	Joins Torpedo School Ship HMS *Vernon*
24 Aug. 1893	Joins HMS *Vulcan*
1895	Joins Torpedo School Ship HMS *Defiance*
18 Aug. 1896	Joins HMS *Empress of India*
1897	Joins HMS *Jupiter*
21 July 1897	Joins HMS *Majestic*
27 Oct. 1897	Death of father
1898	Death of brother
25 May 1900	Appointed to command the National Antarctic Expedition
20 June 1900	Commander
1901	Becomes Freemason

Chronology

31 July 1901	Sails in *Discovery* for Antarctic
16 Aug. 1901	Appointed MVO
10 Sept. 1904	Returns from Antarctic
	Captain
11 Oct. 1904	Advanced to CVO
12 Oct. 1905	Publishes *The Voyage of the 'Discovery'*
	Receives honorary doctorates of science
	from Cambridge and Manchester
1 Dec. 1905	Assistant Director, Naval Intelligence
21 Aug. 1906	Joins HMS *Victorious*
1 Jan. 1907	Joins HMS *Albemarle*
11 Feb. 1907	Collision at sea
25 Aug. 1907	Leaves *Albemarle* on half-pay
25 Jan. 1908	Joins HMS *Essex*
30 May 1908	Joins HMS *Bulwark*
2 Sept. 1908	Marries Kathleen Bruce
	Appointed naval assistant to the
	Second Sea Lord
14 Sept. 1909	Birth of son
2 Dec. 1909	Goes on half-pay to form second
	Antarctic expedition
29 Nov. 1910	Sails from New Zealand in *Terra Nova*
	for the Antarctic
1 Nov. 1911	Leads assault on the South Pole
18 Jan. 1912	Arrives at South Pole and starts return
	journey
29 Mar. 1912	Last journal entry
30 Mar. 1912	Presumed date of death
1913	*Scott's Last Expedition* published
	posthumously

O N E

THE CADET CAPTAIN

Robert Falcon Scott was born on 6 June 1868, in the parish of Stoke Damerel at Devonport, a southern suburb of Plymouth and a thoroughly appropriate birthplace for a boy virtually destined from the cradle for a career in the Navy. The sights and smells of Plymouth Sound would have made some of the earliest impressions on his consciousness, and by an extraordinary chance, a retired Royal Naval assistant paymaster who accompanied Scott on his ill-fated expedition to the South Pole as a meteorologist was actually named Francis Drake.

Robert was always known by his family as Con, an abbreviation of his second name, which in itself seems to have been something of a flight of fancy, although no more of a romantic notion than the family's insistence upon a distant relationship to the novelist Sir Walter Scott. If this connection did exist it was distant in every respect, for there were no literary leanings among Con's immediate forebears. His paternal grandfather, Robert

Scott, had been a naval purser, and on retirement he had become a partner with his brother in a brewery in Plymouth, Scott & Co., purchased for £4,782 out of prize money received during the Napoleonic wars. The brewery was eventually inherited by Con's father, John Edward Scott, the youngest of a family of eight, most of whom sought their fortunes overseas. One of Con's paternal uncles became a surgeon in the Royal Navy, while three others joined that invaluable nineteenth-century standby, the Indian Army.

John Scott inherited not only his father's brewery but a house called Outlands, where he lived in modest comfort with his wife Hannah, the daughter of William Bennett Cuming, a Lloyds surveyor; they married in 1861. Hannah's was a Plymouth family too, with plenty of sea in their veins; one of Con's maternal uncles, Harry, even became an admiral.[1] John and Hannah produced in quick succession a respectable Victorian brood of six children. By the time Con was born in 1868 there were already two girls, Ettie and Rose. Another girl, Grace, followed Con, and when Con was only two years old he was presented with a brother, Archie. There was a fourth girl, Katherine.[2]

In the early years of Con's life profits from the brewery were quite adequate to enable John Scott to support a wife and six children, a commodious house, a carriage and pair, servants and a 2 acre garden with a paddock and outhouses. It was only to be expected that

John would sit on the local bench as a Justice of the Peace, serve as a churchwarden and take an active interest in local politics. But it is said he had to decline an invitation to stand for parliament as a Conservative because he could not afford the expense. The truth is, he was bored by business and fancied himself as a full-time country gentleman, so, most unfortunately as it turned out, he sold the brewery, believing he could indulge his love of gardening on the reinvested proceeds.

While it was customary for middle-class Victorian girls to be educated at home it was rare for a boy not to be sent to boarding school, but Con, allegedly delicate when young, lingered at home too, under the tutelage of a governess. However, when he was eight Con was at last sent as a day-boy to a local school called Exmouth House, making the short journey each day on horseback. Under the influence of his nautical relatives, he began to evince a serious interest in the Navy, and after a few years he was removed to Stubbington House School at Fareham in Hampshire, a preparatory school where it was hoped he would improve academically enough to pass the Royal Navy's cadetship exams.[3] This he succeeded in doing in 1881, at the age of thirteen, and on 15 July that year he joined HMS *Britannia*.

Until he was thirteen, Con's life had been spent largely in female company. His maternal grandparents and a great-aunt had been given a home at Outlands; he had four sisters and only one brother; and he had been taught by a woman, no doubt cheaper than a male tutor. Of his parents, his mother was undoubtedly the dominant character. Now Con was thrust into exactly the kind of male-orientated society he would have inhabited at a public school, but without even the softening influence of a matron or a housemaster's wife. There is no evidence that Scott formed any serious commitment to a woman other than his mother before his marriage, at the relatively late age of forty; his family and educational environments were in fact exactly tailored to suit the repressed conditions necessary to sustain long celibate tours of duty at sea, and eventually years of deprivation as an explorer, always in the sole company of men.

Con's father now had to find annual fees of £100 to support him through his four terms of cadet training, a sum considerably in excess of boarding fees at most public schools before the turn of the century. But despite occasional lapses in good behaviour, and two references to inattentiveness in his conduct sheet, he repaid his father's sacrifice, for in the spring of 1883 he was chosen as Cadet Captain. While on half-holiday on 19 October 1881 Con committed a common schoolboy offence; he trespassed in an orchard. More seriously, on 1 December 1882 he is recorded as having damaged a library book. In April the following year he strayed out of bounds, and on 19 April, 'as Cadet Captain', he allowed some of the other cadets 'to humbug' one of the officers.

It seems as though, in view of his appointment as Cadet Captain, Con exhibited early signs of leadership, not uncommon among rather solitary, even dreamy, boys. The comment 'Inattentive in the Lecture Room while at Study', made on 17 March 1883, was followed seven weeks later by 'Very inattentive in Study'.[4] Yet for two of his four terms Con's study was rated 'satisfactory', for the other two, 'very satisfactory'. Despite his youthful pranks and occasional misdemeanours his general conduct was consistently rated 'very good'. As for his appearance, at thirteen, dressed in a jaunty uniform sparkling with brass buttons, clasping a sword and wearing a fetching naval cap, Robert Scott looked a most engaging lad. He was not especially good-looking or particularly tall but he was sturdy, with an absolutely honest face.

The *Britannia*, a three-decker sailing ship, was moored off Dartmouth. Training was strenuous but humane, and the cadets were permitted adequate leave. They were, after all, only children, and for Con it was easy to get home to Outlands and show off his uniform. It cannot be said that the educational curriculum was wide-ranging. Seamanship was naturally considered vital. Sufficient mathematics were instilled to ensure safe navigation, along with elementary physics, astronomy, geometry and trigonometry. It was no schooling for a boy with artistic interests. Rudimentary French, at which Con was only rated 'fair', was taught, in case the boys landed up in a foreign port where the natives failed to comprehend English. Otherwise, it was assumed that as the boys were aspiring officers and gentlemen they would be most unlikely to want to read for pleasure; rather than study the classics it was thought more important they learn how to toast the queen. Despite an apparent desire to fool around, Con managed to justify his rank as Cadet Captain by coming a respectable seventh in a class of twenty-six, gaining first-class certificates in mathematics and seamanship and a second-class certificate in French. Hence on 24 July 1883, at the age of fifteen, he was posted to the Cape Squadron's flagship, HMS *Boadicea*, becoming a midshipman three weeks later.

The status of a midshipman was a precarious one at the best of times, for although a midshipman was the equivalent of a second lieutenant in the Army, no Army officer would have been commissioned under the age of eighteen, and no fifteen-year-old midshipman could bank on the automatic respect of hardened and experienced able seamen. *Boadicea* was an armoured corvette with a ship's company of nearly 450, so there was no shortage of companionship; quite the reverse. The cramped accommodation would have served as a useful experience for future Antarctic exploration. As a midshipman, Scott continued to receive schooling while training, drilling and taking his turn at keeping watch. As Scott's pay was about £30 a year it was hardly surprising, as his captain noted, that he served 'with sobriety'. A brief spell in a brig, the *Liberty*, caused his second captain to report that Scott was 'a zealous and painstaking young officer'. On 19 September 1885 Scott again transferred, this time to HMS *Monarch*, a third-class battleship attached to the Channel Squadron. On 1 November 1886 he moved on yet again and joined HMS *Rover*, a training ship in which he was to broaden his horizons in more ways than one.

In the first instance, *Rover* transported Scott to the West Indies, where he gained valuable experience racing the three other ships of the training squadron under sail. The second bonus attached to this particular posting was that a guest aboard the squadron's flagship, HMS *Active*, was the man destined to exercise the decisive influence on Scott's life, a man so restlessly active himself that he could not have been enjoying himself aboard a more appropriately named vessel. His name was Clements Markham.

Born in 1830, Markham had gone to sea at fourteen, at a time when sailors were still flogged for drunkenness or disobedience, and according to one of Scott's biographers, Elspeth Huxley, Markham's admiral took with him to the Pacific his wife, four daughters, his six-year-old son and a cow.[5] As a midshipman, in 1850 Markham had joined the search for the missing Arctic explorer Sir John Franklin. He loved the sea but resigned his commission when he was twenty-two in order to explore Peru. He was to become an astonishingly prolific author, penning some fifty volumes of biography and historical romance in addition to ethnographical works. For the past twenty-three years he had served as an honorary secretary of the Royal Geographical Society. And in 1875 he had persuaded Disraeli's government to sponsor a new expedition to the Arctic, with which he sailed as far as Greenland.

But now it was the possibility of exploring the Antarctic that exercised Markham's mind; practically nothing was known of the region whatsoever. Markham felt convinced the task was essentially one for a sailor, for without naval skills no scientists would ever manage to land. He believed too that membership of such an expedition should be confined to the young. He himself could only hope to dream, plan, prod and recruit.

It was while the training squadron lay off St Kitts that Markham first noticed Scott, who on 1 March 1887 found himself in the spotlight after winning a race in the *Rover*'s cutter. The immediate upshot was an invitation to the eighteen-year-old Con Scott to dine aboard *Active*, specifically to meet Mr Markham. Although married, Markham had a penchant for handsome young men, and there were plenty of other midshipmen in the squadron who took it in turns to flit in and out of Markham's favour. Nevertheless, at dinner he was much taken by Scott's 'intelligence, information and the charm of his manner'.[6]

Markham remained with the training squadron for five months, observing the prowess and the charms of all the midshipmen, and the idea frequently put about that at this early stage Markham had marked out Scott as the future leader of an Antarctic expedition has been part of the mythology surrounding Scott, highlighting his abilities and portraying Markham as a salty old sea dog only intent on furthering the careers of the most deserving youngsters.

The squadron dropped anchor off Portland in May 1887. Scott enjoyed home leave at Outlands, and having been promoted acting sub-lieutenant he was posted to the naval college at Greenwich, where in the glorious environment created by Wren he obtained a first-class certificate in seamanship. As a confirmed sub-lieutenant he now joined HMS *Excellent* in order to qualify in gunnery.

Late in 1888 Scott received orders to report for duties to HMS *Amphion*, a cruiser stationed near Vancouver. The journey was not without its incidents. Scott was obliged to make his way as best he could across North America, and for the final leg of the journey, from San Francisco to Esquimault, British Columbia, he joined a tramp steamer bound for Alaska, brim full of women and children as well as men bound for the Alaskan mines. As luck would have it, the boat ran into a storm, whereupon most of the men took to the bottle and the stewards to their cabins. This left Scott to organize the women and children, which he appears to have done with singular skill, 'dressing the mothers', according to a possibly slightly embroidered version of events later penned by a fellow passenger, a 23-year-old Old Etonian by the name of Courtauld Thomson,[7] washing the children, feeding the babies, scrubbing down the floors and nursing the sick, performing, in fact, 'every imaginable service for all hands'.

Amphion was a second-class cruiser, in which Scott was to traverse the Mediterranean and the Pacific, no longer confined to a hammock but in theory the fortunate occupant of a cabin. But he was not a happy young man, reporting to his father that he was cold, dirty, slightly seasick, very homesick, hungry and tired. To add to his woes, the wardroom was 'upside down' and his cabin 'chaotic and stuffy'.[8] But serving on such a seemingly ill-run ship as *Amphion* did not impede Scott's automatic climb up the ladder. With his promotion to lieutenant gazetted on 14 August 1889 he now decided to specialize in torpedoes, and he was given permission to join a Torpedo School Ship, HMS *Vernon*, stationed at Portsmouth. The problem of homesickness would have been solved, at any rate.

A torpedo in Scott's day was not discharged submerged from a submarine, a vessel yet to be designed. It was a weapon fired from the deck. By the time Scott began his training there were some 200 torpedo boats in the British Navy, all part of a growing

escalation of war at sea. The torpedo boat was intended
to harry cumbersome warships, and in order to pursue
the torpedo boats a new, lighter warship, later known as
a destroyer, came into operation. However, Scott was
not to live to take part in the great sea battles of the
First World War in which these developments were put
to such effective use.

Scott remained at Portsmouth until 24 August 1893,
when he returned to the Mediterranean, as torpedo
lieutenant on HMS *Vulcan*, a ship still undergoing trials.
Some were sceptical about *Vulcan's* many-faceted roles.
She was part cruiser, part repair ship, and more or less a
floating torpedo depot and dockyard. But Scott thought
his ship 'a splendid but under-developed and misused
experiment', and told his father the experience he was
gaining was just as good as any he would have achieved
on a battleship. With a touch of exuberant youthful
pride he informed John Scott, 'I look upon myself now
as an authority on the only modern way of working a
minefield'.[9]

But just as Scott seemed settled on a promising and
much more satisfying naval career, domestic disaster
struck. The capital invested from the sale of Scott & Co.
had been lost, and with it the modest income John Scott
thought had set him free to enjoy the cultivation of his
garden. In October 1894 both garden and house had to
be let, and at the age of sixty-three John Scott was
forced to seek employment. 'A crushing blow came &

heavy losses', Hannah Scott wrote in her diary. 'From Con comes a fine manly reliable letter offering help.'[10]

Con's reaction to his parent's misfortune was instinctive and typical. He was by no means well off himself – it was difficult for an officer to live on his pay alone, and he had no private income – but he contributed what he could to make ends meet at home. Rose immediately left Outlands to take up nursing in Nottingham, and it was not long before Ettie, too, had flown the nest, although not perhaps in the direction her religious martinet of a mother would have wished; she joined a touring company which boasted the august membership of Irene Vanbrugh. Grace and Kate set up as dressmakers in London, while Archie's efforts to help his parents were the most self-sacrificing of all. In order to cut down his own expenses and have more money to send home, Archie transferred to an unsmart regiment in Nigeria.[11]

The situation seemed so desperate that Con asked for a transfer from *Vulcan* to another Torpedo School Ship, HMS *Defiance*. *Defiance* was based at Devonport, and Con would therefore be on hand to help settle his parents into new accommodation near Shepton Mallet, where his father had found employment as manager of a local brewery.

It was nine years since Scott had first met Clements Markham, but now, once again, their paths were to cross. Chafing at a shore posting, in August 1896 Scott managed to have himself transferred to the *Empress of India*, a first-class ironclad seagoing ship. She was part of the Channel Squadron, and was soon heading for a cruise to Gibraltar, during the course of which Scott dressed up in drag to play the principal lady in a play called *Bombastes Furioso*. His mother was informed that he wore a 'gorgeous golden wig' complete with a dress, made on board, stays, silk stockings and buckled shoes. He appears to have been equally pleased with his 'rich falsetto voice'.[12]

On board the *Empress of India's* sister ship, the *Royal Sovereign*, was Markham, recently appointed president of the Royal Geographical Society and invested by Queen Victoria as a Knight Commander of the Order of the Bath, an unexpected honour for a man who might reasonably have expected a modest knight bachelor-hood. Markham remembered Scott, and they conversed amiably enough, but by no stretch of the imagination could Scott at this stage be said to have shared what, for Markham, had become a passion, plans to explore the Antarctic. Markham's suggestion that the Admiralty should organise an expedition had already been turned down, but he was determined to renew the onslaught, and was busy lecturing and firing off letters to try to whip up enthusiasm. Eventually his conversation was to ignite at least a spark of interest in Scott.

It was half a century since Captain James Clark Ross, after whom the Ross Sea was named, had sighted the range of mountains he called the Great Ice Barrier, and still no one knew what lay beyond, whether indeed the Antarctic was a continent. The lack of reliable navigational aids and maps, and the ever constant threat of disaster from ice packs and icebergs, had not prevented seal hunters from venturing into these largely uncharted waters, but Markham grew daily crosser at the lack of any official interest in following up the early British expedition led by Ross. It was Ross who in 1831 had planted the British flag at the North Magnetic Pole; Sir Clements Markham was quite determined that a British subject should be the first to reach the South Pole.[13]

DEPLORABLE IGNORANCE

Early in 1897 Robert Scott enjoyed a brief tour of duty on a battleship, HMS *Jupiter* (his naval postings were nothing if not varied and frequent), soon transferring to *Jupiter*'s sister ship, HMS *Majestic*, flagship of the Channel Squadron. *Majestic* was a modern ironclad that had cost the Treasury £900,000; she was equipped with four 12-inch guns and torpedoes mounted below decks as well as on, and was well ahead in design of any foreign battleship afloat at the time. It was among the 700-strong crew of the *Majestic* that Scott came into contact with royalty for the first time. His captain was Prince Louis of Battenberg,[1] the 43-year-old husband of Queen Victoria's granddaughter, Princess Victoria of Hesse.

In spite of the size of the ship's complement Scott must, if only subconsciously, have been keeping his eyes peeled for exceptional talent; it was from friendships made on *Majestic* that for his first Antarctic expedition he recruited two lieutenants, Michael Barne (who, like

Scott, had been a boy at Stubbington House School) and Reginald Skelton, Warrant Officer James Dellbridge (as second engineer), and a couple of Petty Officers, Edgar Evans (who was to lose his life on the second expedition) and David Allan.

However, after only four months afloat the fun of serving under a prince and on such a magnificent ship was overshadowed; on 27 October 1897 Scott's father succumbed to heart disease and dropsy. He was only sixty-six; and he only left £1,545. Once again, Hannah Scott was reduced to near penury. Because of service duties, neither Con nor Archie were able to attend their father's funeral. When at last the brothers were reunited they managed to raise an annual allowance of £200 for their mother. Luckily, Con gained permission for his brother to accompany him in *Majestic* on a cruise to Ireland – luckily because it was to be the last stretch of time they would ever spend together. Just a year after John Scott's death, Archie contracted typhoid, that scourge of Victorian England (it had carried off the Prince Consort himself), and died.

Born and bred to preserve a stiff upper lip under all adversity, Scott wrote to his mother from Gibraltar to say he was glad Archie had suffered no pain – and it was easy to understand that he died like a man. As he earned more than Con, Archie had been providing two-thirds of his mother's allowance. Now that he was dead, Con faced a pretty desperate situation, both financially and emotionally. In a family of five women he was now the only male, with a triple burden of responsibility; to maintain morale, to provide an income, and to excel in such a way as to uphold single-handed the family honour. Some way had to be found of gaining swifter promotion than peacetime service might normally afford, and it was a third chance encounter with Sir Clements Markham that finally changed the entire course of Scott's life and determined his destiny.

Markham was on his way down Buckingham Palace Road to his house, No. 21 Eccleston Square, one summer day in 1899 when Scott, who was to set up home in Buckingham Palace Road after his marriage, spied the great man, crossed the road and followed him. The previous year Markham had published a pamphlet entitled *Antarctic Exploration: A Plea for a National Expedition*. But his plea had fallen largely on deaf ears. He reckoned £50,000 would be required, and until a few days ago he had been promised a mere £14,000. But a generous donation of £25,000 from a wealthy industrialist had finally shamed the Treasury into promising financial assistance, and it was an optimistic and excited Clements Markham who was able to tell Scott that he thought a British Antarctic Expedition was a real possibility.

Two days later, Lieutenant Robert Scott applied to lead the expedition. Considering that in his account of the expedition, *The Voyage of the 'Discovery'*, he was to write, 'I had no predilection for polar exploration',[2] it seems an odd thing for Scott to have done almost on the spur of the moment. But Scott was serving as a naval officer at a time when private wealth and social rank, neither of which he possessed, were as likely to ensure promotion as competence at one's job, and with Markham's backing he must have seen in a flash a way to prove that he could make a success of his life – even achieve fame – without the benefits of money and influential family connections.

Scott had to sail the Mediterranean in *Majestic* for a further year while a joint committee from the Royal Geographical Society, which had previously sponsored explorers like Burton and Livingstone, and the Royal Society – the national academy of science granted its Charter by Charles II in 1662 – bickered among themselves, discussing, among other matters, the relative merits of four other contenders for leadership of an expedition. Eventually, on 25 May 1900, Scott's appointment as commander of the National Antarctic Expedition was signed by Markham, and a month later Scott was promoted to Commander. (The rank of lieutenant-commander did not exist until 1914.)

Whether the expedition committee remained quite so thrilled with their choice of the 32-year-old Commander Scott on receipt of a list of demands, almost certainly dictated by Markham, may be doubted. Scott told them in no uncertain terms that he wanted 'complete command of the ship and landing parties', and he insisted on being consulted over 'all future appointments, both civilian and others, especially the doctor'. He listed his demands under six heads, the sixth stating bluntly: 'I am ready to insist on these conditions to the point of resignation if, in my opinion, their refusal imperils the success of the undertaking.'[3] He could afford to resign; the Admiralty had seconded him on full pay.

Scott had less than a year in which to plan the expedition from scratch, to select officers and men, to purchase provisions, and to study previous experience of travel by sledge. 'My room [in Burlington House] soon became a veritable museum of curiosities', he wrote. 'Sledges, ski, fur clothing and boots were crowded into the corners, whilst tables and shelves were littered with correspondence and innumerable samples of tinned foods.'[4] He travelled to Norway with Clements Markham to pick the brains of an experienced explorer, Fridtjof Nansen, who wrote of Scott afterwards, 'I see him before me, his tight, wiry figure, his intelligent, handsome face, the earnest, fixed look, and those expressive lips so seriously determined and yet ready to smile'.[5]

By the end of 1900 Scott was so frustrated at continually having to refer decisions to a committee of thirty-two assorted hagglers that he asked for, and obtained, permission to work on his own to an agreed budget. It was soon realized that Markham's original belief that the expedition could be financed for £50,000 was wide of the mark. A new wooden ship being built by the Dundee Ship Building Company, and to be christened *Discovery*, was to cost £50,000 alone, and in the event £93,000 was subscribed. A nephew of Markham, Lieutenant Charles Royds, was taken on as meteorologist, and Scott had foisted on him by the newspaper proprietor Alfred Harmsworth, as his navigator and second-in-command, a P&O Line officer four years older than himself, Lieutenant Albert Armitage. Harmsworth, later Lord Northcliffe, had donated £5,000 on condition that two of his nominees were appointed.

Armitage fell for Scott's charm, and later recalled:

> I consented to go even though it was against my better reasoning. Scott had no understanding of the work that he was undertaking; I had three years knowledge of it. [Armitage had served in the Arctic between 1894–6 as nautical astronomer to the Jackson-Harmsworth expedition to Franz Josef Land, which was why he was already known to Harmsworth.] I was to be his adviser, a sort of dry-nurse, and knew enough of human nature to fear the result.

But he had to admit that he had never worked with a more delightful man than Scott.[6]

Albert Armitage was clearly a man of honour. The majority of the committee were scientists and many would have preferred that Scott was merely captain of the *Discovery*, not in overall charge of the expedition. When Armitage was secretly approached to see whether, if Scott could be persuaded to resign, he would be prepared to take over, he indignantly declined. But both Scott and Markham came very near to resigning. Scott asked his second-in-command to call at the house in Chelsea – No. 80 Hospital Road – where he was lodging with his mother. 'Things are now in a condition from which I can see no way out but resignation', Scott wrote. 'I should be glad therefore to explain the situation to you.' In the event, Armitage and Markham managed to restore Scott's self-confidence and dissuaded him from taking any drastic action. This was just as well for Hannah Scott. As commander of the expedition Scott was to be paid £500 a year on top of his naval salary, and Hannah was able to tell her son, 'You have surrounded me with all the comfort I can possibly want'.[7]

The *Discovery*, 172 ft long, 34 ft in breadth and with a registered tonnage of 485, was launched by Lady Markham on 21 March 1901. After sea trials she arrived at the East India Docks on 6 June. It is small wonder that many photographs taken on board ship show the table laden with bottles. Among the cargo stowed away were 22 gallons of brandy, another 27 gallons of whisky, 60 cases of port, 36 of sherry and 28 of champagne. Much of this beverage was reserved for birthdays, thoughtfully noted down in a wardroom book by Markham, but a good deal of it was actually returned to England untouched. Scott himself was almost teetotal and many of the other members of the expedition surprisingly abstemious. (Scott's second Antarctic expedition was presented with 35,000 cigars!)

Having released four lieutenants to serve under Scott the Admiralty said enough was enough, and as his third officer Scott had recommended to him a young Irishman of twenty-seven, an officer with the Union Castle Line, Ernest Shackleton. It had been the father of one of Shackleton's passengers who had so recently donated £25,000 to the expedition, and who now put forward Shackleton's name. Once again Scott found his hands tied by financial considerations. But whatever the slightly dubious merits of Shackleton's initial engagement, he was eventually to establish a reputation at least as illustrious as that of Scott himself. He was extraordinarily brave and resourceful and as brilliant at financing expeditions as he was at leading them. He become so famous that his memorial service at St Paul's Cathedral in 1922 was attended by George V and Queen Mary.[8]

Another significant choice for Scott's first expedition, as assistant surgeon, was Dr Edward Wilson, twenty-nine years of age and a man of many parts, a recently qualified doctor, a zoologist and a competent water-colourist. When he and Scott first met, Wilson was still recovering from a painful abscess under his armpit and had his arm in a sling. Scott took to him at once. The fact that Wilson had previously spent two years fighting pulmonary tuberculosis deterred neither Scott nor Wilson himself, even when an Admiralty medical board pronounced him unfit. Wilson is always said to have been Scott's greatest friend. Scott certainly needed Wilson to complement his own personality in a number of ways. For instance, Scott felt no serious allegiance to religion, and Wilson's deeply ingrained Christian faith – he was a kind of Franciscan fatalist – in part accounted for the attraction. It is indicative of male friendships at that time that invariably in his journals Scott refers to Edward Wilson as Wilson, and only called him Bill when writing a farewell letter to Wilson's wife as the two lay dying in their tent.

With so much critical planning on hand, Scott still found time, in April 1901, to be initiated as a Freemason. He and his officers were also easily enticed to a grand send-off dinner at the Savage Club. In order to regularize Scott's entries in the Navy List while he was away he was formally posted to HMS *President*, a drill ship of the Royal Naval Reserve, and, having selected for his reading matter on the journey south Charles Darwin's *Origin of Species* in preference to any number of up-to-date works on polar travel, Scott took *Discovery*, the sixth ship so named in the past 300 years and the first ship he had ever commanded, down the

Thames. He had a crew of forty-four, whose average age was twenty-five; his brief was to follow in the wake of Captain Ross, to winter on the coast of Victoria Land, and, more precisely, to 'determine, as far as possible, the nature, condition and extent of that portion of the South Polar lands' included in the scope of his expedition. He was also to make a magnetic survey of the southern regions to the south of the 40th parallel and 'to carry on meteorological, oceanographical, geological, biological and physical investigations and researches'.[9] In other words, Scott's was a scientific expedition, and it was made clear to him that scientific study was not to be sacrificed in the interests of exploration. Scott had the Victorian layman's natural fascination with science, and to him such instructions would have made perfect sense.

In an age of leisurely activity, *Discovery* first of all found time to look in at the Cowes Regatta, where she and her crew were honoured by a visit from the king. Edward VII was in many ways an imaginative monarch, and he had been thoroughly enjoying the first heady six months of his long-delayed reign. Clearly he felt that much national prestige was invested in the expedition, and that its leader should carry with him into the unknown some symbol of his Sovereign's confidence and support – a kind of good luck talisman. The ubiquitous Order of the British Empire had not yet been instituted, and Scott was scarcely eligible at this stage of his naval career to be awarded the Order of the Bath. In any case, to have conferred a CB on Scott would have meant obtaining at short notice the consent of the prime minister. However, within Edward's own prerogative was the Order founded just five years previously by his mother, and so the monarch duly conferred on Scott Membership of the Royal Victorian Order, his appointment being gazetted on 16 August 1901.

Ill prepared in many vital matters, Scott was to learn as he went along, and one of his first disquieting discoveries, in the Bay of Biscay, was that he would be lucky to get more than 6 knots out of *Discovery*. Worse still, although *Discovery* was brand new, she leaked because of poor workmanship. She required a month in dock at Lyttelton in New Zealand, during which time damaged stock had also to be replaced. When eventually they sailed, on Christmas Eve, on deck was a flock of forty-five sheep together with twenty-three dogs – a somewhat incompatible cargo, surely. One is left wondering why the sheep had not been slaughtered and the meat frozen for the journey instead of the animals taking up valuable space, making a filthy mess and being subjected to a rough sea voyage. It almost beggars belief that Scott had failed to take with him any food with fat content for the dogs, relying instead on a diet of frozen fish, most of which went bad. The work the dogs were expected to do proved totally beyond them anyway, and the tale of how they fell down dead or had to be destroyed and fed to their companions makes horrific reading. A dog is a pack animal, and Scott had no rapport with dogs whatsoever, believing that if they were whipped they would lead. Had Scott merely walked ahead, or better still skied ahead, they would have followed.

'As may be imagined,' Scott wrote in his account of the journey, 'the ship was not in a condition in which one could look forward with pleasure to crossing the stormiest ocean in the world.' With stalwart optimism he trusted 'that providence would vouchsafe to us fine weather and an easy passage to the south'.[10] And providence itself, in the person of the Bishop of Christchurch, turned up to wish them God speed. But God moves in very mysterious ways indeed, sometimes ignoring even the prayers of bishops, and as the waving crowds on shore were vanishing into the distance an over-excited (some said intoxicated) young seaman called Charles Bonner, a lad everyone liked, climbed above the crow's nest, stood up to return the waves and fell to his death.

With the deck already overcrowded and the boat dangerously overloaded, Scott called in at Port Chalmers to take on board a gift of another 45 tons of coal. On 3 January 1902, ten days out from New Zealand, *Discovery* crossed the Antarctic Circle. With time on his hands to write home, Edward Wilson reported to his father that the only thing about Scott he did not admire was his temper. Otherwise he was 'thoughtful for each individual and does little kindnesses which show'. He was also 'very definite about everything'. Hence there would be 'no fear of our wandering about aimlessly in the Southern regions'.[11]

There was every danger, however. After four days of fighting her way through pack ice, *Discovery* found herself in open sea, and Scott gave orders to splice the mainbrace. But it was not long before they were being buffeted by winds of 90 mph. At various temporary landing spots the crew left tin cylinders containing information about their route, hopefully to be picked up by a relief ship Sir Clements Markham was prudently planning to send out the following year.

While still searching for permanent winter quarters, Scott named a particularly bleak stretch of rocks King Edward VII Land. Safe moorings were eventually found on the shore of McMurdo Sound, and Scott wrote in his somewhat stilted style:

> Repeated walks are taken to the hill-tops in the immediate vicinity, and eyes are turned towards the south – the land of promise. Many are the arguments as to what lies in the misty distance, and as to what obstacles the spring journeys will bring to light.[12]

Navigating a ship was something Scott had been trained to do from an early age. What he knew of life ashore in the Antarctic would scarcely have covered the back of a postage stamp. He later acknowledged:

> I am bound to confess that the sledges when packed presented an appearance of which we should afterwards have been wholly ashamed, and much the same might be said of the clothing worn by the sledgers. But at this time our ignorance was deplorable.[13]

He admitted they had no idea what food to take, how to use their cookers or how to erect their tents – 'or even how to put on our clothes'. Not a single item of their equipment had been tested. The dogs proved to be unmanageable cannibals, a steward broke a leg, and Markham's nephew very nearly drowned. The ultimate outcome of this fiasco was that all the dogs and one man were lost.

The first exploratory sledging party returned after three days suffering from frostbite for they had marched until exhausted in a snowstorm. A second party consisting of four officers and eight men fared even worse. Provided with too few pairs of skis, three of the officers continued alone, sending the eight men and one officer back to the ship. Leaving their tents in a blizzard they continued the return trek and suddenly found themselves on the edge of a precipice. Two men hurtled over, one to his death. The other had a miraculous escape, eventually crawling home on his hands and knees.

Scott had good cause for pessimism. 'Our autumn sledging was at an end,' he recalled in the account published on his return, 'and left me with much food for thought. In one way or another each journey had been a failure. . . . It was clear there would have to be a thorough reorganisation before the spring.'[14]

It is disturbing to find at this time a young physicist, Louis Bernacchi, a Tasmanian and a graduate of Melbourne University, writing of Scott: 'Mentally he could do a lot of work, swiftly and clearly, but he could be lazy, too, at times, and slip into moods of silence and contemplation.' Echoing Wilson's impression, Bernacchi added, 'He certainly could be irritable and impatient'.[15] Notwithstanding his criticisms, in 1906 Bernacchi was to ask Scott to be best man at his wedding.

Clearly determined to win glory for himself and possibly an early demise, Scott decided to lead a trek south, planning, at first, to take only one companion. Eventually he had the sense to take two, but returned two days later having endured a hair-raising experience when they failed to secure their tent properly; the temperature dropped to –50 degrees and the result was frostbite.

Nothing daunted, Scott set out again, accompanied by Ernest Shackleton and a boatswain called Thomas Feather. Marking the spot with a black flag, they laid a depot containing provisions for a six-week period 85 miles south of *Discovery*. Problems persisted. Feather fell down a crevasse, and was fortunately rescued by Scott, who returned to *Discovery* to receive the appalling news that the crew had fallen prey to scurvy. Shackleton was eventually to suffer so badly that against his will he was sent home on the relief ship.

On 2 November, accompanied by Wilson and Shackleton, Scott plunged into a journey south much as the Light Brigade had tackled the Russian guns – in a spirit of British pragmatism and pointless heroics. Wilson was afflicted by agonizing snow blindness, and the return march bore all the hallmarks of a dress rehearsal for the fatal events of 1912. Although exhausted, they marched in a blizzard, desperately hungry and with Shackleton spitting blood. Having finally lost every single dog they had set out with, Scott and Wilson were reduced to pulling the sledges themselves, for Shackleton was too ill. With immense good fortune they reached each food depot with a day to spare, and by the time they struggled back to the ship they had covered 960 miles in ninety-three days.

In Scott's absence, Albert Armitage had found an entrance through the coastal mountains to the inner ice plateau of Victoria Land, discovering, in fact, the Antarctic Ice Cap. And Sir Clements Markham's relief ship, *Morning*, had arrived. Aboard, as second officer, was a young lieutenant with the resounding name of Edward Ratcliffe Garth Russell Evans, who in 1910 was to return to the Antarctic as Scott's second-in-command.

In September 1903 Scott organized three exploratory parties, all with orders to report back to *Discovery* by mid-December. He himself was to lead a trek to the high ice plateau behind the coastal region. Again they encountered blizzards and, at night, temperatures of –50 degrees, which was nothing compared to the cold experienced by another party; –70 degrees. Six days after Scott's party had set out, their sledges, weighed down with 200 tons of food and equipment, broke down and the group had to return to base for repairs to be carried out by the resident carpenter. The next set-back graphically illustrates the primitive conditions under which the team were working, as well as their lack of knowledge and experience. Thanks to a gale, they managed to lose a handbook supplied by the Royal Geographical Society, called *Hints to Travellers*, which contained vital explanations for explorers, bereft of landmarks, as to how to work out latitude and longitude by observing the sun and stars – knowledge one would surely have expected these men to have had without the need to refer to a manual.

'The gravity of this blow', Scott recorded, 'can scarcely be exaggerated.' After everyone in the party had agreed to take the risk, it was decided to push on rather than return to the ship a second time. So they climbed to a height of 7,000 ft, where the gale subjected them to frostbite, yet they managed at last to dig in and erect three tents. 'Nothing but experience saved us from disaster today,' Scott recorded before he fell asleep exhausted, 'for I feel pretty confident that we could not have stood another hour in the open.'[16]

For all his shortcomings Scott had many of the attributes of a true explorer, in particular the need to know what lies around the next corner. Having reached the summit, camping 8,900 ft above sea level, he wrote:

> I do not think that it would be possible to conceive a more cheerless prospect than that which faced us at that time, when on this lofty, desolate plateau we turned our backs upon the last mountain peak that could remind us of habitable lands. Yet before us lay the unknown. What fascination lies in the word! Could anyone wonder that we determined to push on, be the outlook ever so comfortless?'[17]

They were setting out across terrain on which no man had ever set foot. David Livingstone, who died in 1873, had been exploring Africa during Scott's early childhood; now that vast continent was almost entirely opened up. The interior of China remained mysterious but no longer unrecorded. Only the Antarctic waited to reveal its awful secrets to the last amateurishly intrepid successors to a great line of Victorian eccentrics.

T H R E E

NO STONE
UNTURNED

Those of us who seldom venture further than Spain or the south of France, and then in search of warmth and pleasure, may wonder what it was that drove men like Robert Scott and his companions to suffer torture in the cause of exploration, although so far as his first Antarctic expedition was concerned the cynical answer might be that they simply did not know what they were letting themselves in for. By the time they specifically set out for the South Pole they most certainly did.

Scott wrote in 1903, in a temperature of −40 degrees:

> The wind is the plague of our lives. It has cut us to pieces. We all have deep cracks in our nostrils and cheeks, and our lips are broken and raw, our fingers are also getting in a shocking state; one of Evans's thumbs has a deep cut on either side of the nail which might have been made by a heavy slash with a knife. We can do nothing for this so long as we have to face this horrid wind.[1]

Eventually, on reaching the summit of the high ice plateau behind the coastal region, and realizing there was nothing beyond 'but a further expanse of our terrible plateau', Scott admitted they had reached the end of their tether. 'And all we have done is show the immensity of this vast plain.' He described the scene as 'so wildly and awfully desolate that it cannot fail to impress one with gloomy thoughts'.[2]

Introspective at the best of times, Scott was now obviously depressed. 'We, little human insects,' he wrote, 'have started to crawl over this awful desert and are now bent on crawling back again. Could anything be more terrible than this silent, wind-swept immensity when one thinks such thoughts?' At least when, on 1 December, Scott's party headed for home, still in daytime temperatures of −25 degrees, they did so with the wind behind them.

Nevertheless they were fortunate ever to locate *Discovery*. They lost their bearings, and two members of the party, one of them Scott himself, suddenly plunged down a crevasse. It was Christmas Eve when they clambered aboard the ship, having on this occasion hauled their sledges 1,098 miles in eighty-one days. News imparted by the other parties who had been out exploring was equally impressive. The heights of more than 200 mountain peaks had been fixed, photographs had been taken, penguins examined and magnetic data recorded.

Discovery was now well and truly wedged in the ice, and Scott had visions of spending another winter in the Antarctic, existing on a diet of penguin and seal. The same thought had occurred to the ever resourceful Sir Clements Markham, who this time had sent out two relief ships, *Morning*, as before, and her companion the *Terra Nova*. On 5 January 1904 both ships suddenly came into view.

Morning had previously returned to England with dispatches, which included news of the outbreak of scurvy. This had sent the expedition's sponsors into a flat spin. They imagined *Discovery* was about to be abandoned – which indeed, it very nearly was. At first the government refused to help, but then relented, offering a grant of £12,000 on condition that *Morning* was handed over lock, stock and barrel. The prime minister, Arthur Balfour, helpfully weighed in by saying that confidence in the handling of the National Antarctic Expedition had been 'rudely shaken'. And then, even more helpfully, the Admiralty squandered funds they had previously withheld, paying for the second relief ship, *Terra Nova*, eight times more than Markham had paid for *Morning*. One of those who helped prepare *Terra Nova* for her race to the Antarctic (she was towed south to join *Morning* at Hobart, Tasmania, at a speed which 'must have surprised the barnacles on her stout wooden sides', as Scott was to comment) was Ernest Shackleton, most unwillingly invalided home the year before.

When all this palaver was relayed to Scott on board *Discovery* he coolly wrote to one of the organizers of the relief expedition, Vice Admiral Pelham Aldrich, 'I don't think an alarmist view was justifiable on anything I wrote and as a matter of fact we never felt alarm. . . . We passed a most pleasant winter, entirely free from sickness or anxiety.'

Nevertheless, it seemed that *Discovery* was well and truly stuck fast, so equipment was transferred to the two relief vessels. Arrangements to abandon ship were almost complete when unexpectedly the ice began to melt, and by 16 February *Discovery* was once again riding freely at anchor. Back on board came all the specimens and instruments previously transferred to *Morning* and *Terra Nova*.

After taking on as much coal as *Morning* could spare, Scott decided on the way home to explore the region west of Cape Adare. But he was lucky to live to explore anywhere at all. On the point of departure a gale blew up before *Discovery* had managed to clear a shallow patch of water leading to the open sea. In one of those split-second decisions naval officers are sometimes called upon to make, Scott, seeing a strong current rushing past, swung the helm over, and hoping to make a dash for it, steered – or tried to steer – for the open water.

'But the moment the *Discovery's* bows entered the fast-running stream she was swung round like a top and crashed head foremost on to the shoal.'[3] In later tranquillity, Scott was to recall the hours this terrifying episode lasted as 'truly the most dreadful I have ever spent. Each moment the ship came down with a sickening thud which shook her from stem to stern, and each thud seemed to show more plainly, strong as was her build, she could not long survive such awful blows.' She had in fact run aground. 'With the heavier blows', Scott recorded, 'one could see the whole ship temporarily distorted in shape; through all and directly beneath one's feet could be heard the horrible crunching and grinding of the keel on the stones below.'[4]

Just as suddenly as the gale had blown up, it dropped, and *Discovery* managed to escape from the shoal. It was later discovered the rudder had been shattered, and this had to be replaced. The fact that the pumps had ceased to work as well seemed like a minor detail. After some exploratory sailing along the coast of Victoria Land, *Discovery* was finally obliged to head north, and on 5 March 1904 she recrossed the Antarctic Circle, two years and sixty days since her first crossing south. Having met up again with the two relief ships, Scott and his companions arrived back at Lyttelton on 1 April, which happened to be Good Friday. Despite a catalogue of mistakes and disasters, Scott's expedition had travelled 300 miles further south than anyone had been before, to within 480 miles of the Pole, had undertaken twenty-eight perilous sledging journeys, and had returned with a mass of scientific data. It had charted the life history of the Emperor penguin, noted hitherto unknown rock and plant fossils, and made meteorological and magnetic records. Waiting for Scott at Lyttelton was a message of congratulations from the king, and the news that the explorer was to be presented with the Patron's Medal of the Royal Geographical Society.

Better still, to coincide with Scott's arrival at Spithead on 10 September he was promoted to the rank of captain, equivalent to colonel in the Army. *The Times* informed its readers that Captain Scott had navigated the *Discovery* 'with the highest skill and courage in the most difficult circumstances', and that in his role as an explorer he had displayed 'brilliant enterprise, patient perseverance and daring'.[5] Waiting to greet him was the inspirer of the whole expedition, Sir Clements Markham, and a scrummage of excited reporters. The *Daily Express* wrote that the colour of the explorers' faces was 'almost black, like seasoned mahogany', and that their movements were deliberate, 'as though they had long been used to heavy garments that encumbered them'. Interestingly, the paper added that 'all of them spoke in curiously slow voices'.[6]

Seemingly anticipating a return to the Antarctic, Scott told a reporter from the *Daily Mail* that although they had done much in the way of discovery, 'it can only be regarded as a scratch on the ice compared with what is to be done'.[7]

By contrast to the generous hospitality shown to Scott and his friends when they arrived in New Zealand, the City of London could not even be troubled to lay on an official welcome, and the *Daily Mail* commented, 'Had the ship's crew perished in the Antarctic we doubtless should have raised a national memorial to them'. It was once again left to the king to use his personal initiative, and this he did by inviting Scott to stay at Balmoral, where at a quite informal ceremony he advanced him to Commander of the Royal Victorian Order.[8] The prime minister was now claiming credit for 'fathering' the expedition, but he failed even to make Scott a Companion of the Order of the Bath, which in view of his achievements and naval rank would have been an appropriate honour. Scott was back in Scotland a year later, attending the 21st birthday party at Glamis Castle of Patrick Glamis, heir to the 14th Earl of Strathmore and Kinghorne, and it is perfectly possible he set eyes upon the future Queen Elizabeth the Queen Mother, Lord Glamis's youngest sister, then aged five.

Almost as soon as he had returned from the Antarctic, Scott was planning to produce an account of his journey for the benefit of the public, and the result was a book called *The Voyage of the 'Discovery'*. It was published in two volumes, on 12 October 1905, and the terms agreed by Smith, Elder & Co. (they were later taken over by John Murray) were extraordinarily generous. Scott was to receive three-quarters of the royalties, which resulted at the end of 1905 in a cheque for £1,569. With a reckless abandon to match that of his publishers, Scott gave away 100 copies of the book, and insisted on paying Dr Wilson £100 for the use of one of his drawings; all told, the book carried 260 illustrations. Scott's mother and sisters had by now moved to No. 56 Oakley Street, Chelsea, and this was to become Scott's home base for the next four years. But conditions in Chelsea do not seem to have been conducive to writing, and *The Voyage of the 'Discovery'*, which went into a second edition almost straight away, was written partly under Markham's roof at No. 21 Eccleston Square and partly at a hotel in Ashdown.[9]

In preparing his diaries for publication, Scott took the opportunity to gloss over many of his mistakes. Roland Huntford has described *The Voyage of the 'Discovery'* as 'a minor masterpiece of the literature of apologetics', and believes that it sowed the seeds of a legend in the way that *The Seven Pillars of Wisdom* 'created' Lawrence of Arabia.[10]

During this period, Scott also undertook a wearisome series of lectures; his itinerary included Edinburgh, Glasgow, Dundee, Hull, Manchester, Liverpool and Eastbourne, and he acquired the reputation of being one of the fastest speakers on the lecture circuit. The Royal Geographical Society struck a special gold medal in his honour, and not to be outdone, America presented him with the Philadelphia Geographical Society's gold medal for 1904. In 1906 he received the gold medal of the American Geographical Society, and two years later the Berlin Geographical Society presented Scott with its Nachtigal gold medal.[11] The apotheosis of his elevation to fame were honorary doctorates of science conferred on him by the universities of Cambridge and Manchester, and to celebrate all these triumphs he sat for a full-length portrait by Daniel Wehrschmidt (now in the National Portrait Gallery), resplendent in naval full dress uniform with the collar and badge of the CVO round his neck. It was in 1905, too, that in *Vanity Fair* he was caricatured by 'Spy', a sure sign that he had arrived in Society.

On 1 December 1905 Scott was appointed assistant director of naval intelligence at the Admiralty, but by 21 August 1906 he was at sea again, as captain of the battleship *Victorious*. On the first day of 1907 he transferred, again as captain, to a more modern battleship, HMS *Albemarle*, which he very nearly lost on the night of 11 February, in a collision off the coast of Portugal with a sister battleship, *Commonwealth*. The ship in line ahead of *Albemarle* suddenly swung out of formation, and to avoid ramming her, *Albemarle* was obliged to follow on, and in doing so she crashed into *Commonwealth*, coming up behind.

The scene represented 'a picture of helplessness and a possibility of catastrophe which is not easily forgotten,' Scott wrote to his mother. 'It was perhaps some half hour before [*Commonwealth*] reported that there was no danger of sinking.'[12] Scott's ship sustained superficial damage to her bows but the *Commonwealth's* damage was so extensive that she was kept in dry dock for several months. Fortunately for Scott and several others, a court of inquiry more or less wrote off the accident (which could have had fatal consequences) as a natural nautical hazard – a relief indeed for a member of the Naval and Military Club who had left the bridge of his ship at a critical moment in manoeuvres.[13]

It was at a luncheon party in 1906, a few months prior to the collision at sea, that Scott, his mind half on his naval duties, half on dreams of obtaining further fame as an explorer, briefly met his future wife, Kathleen Bruce. She was ten years younger than Scott, the youngest of a family of eleven children (including two sets of twins), who had all been born in such rapid succession that by the time Kathleen made her appearance on 27 March 1878 her mother was completely worn out. She died when Kathleen was only two and a half. Kathleen's father, the Reverend Lloyd Bruce, a canon of York, appears not to have been too grief stricken as nine months later he remarried.

When Kathleen was seven, her father died. Taken pity on by a well-meaning but intimidating great-uncle, the Historiographer Royal of Scotland, and hence a member of Queen Victoria's Household, Kathleen and most of her brothers and sisters were now given an austere home in Edinburgh. But this was not to last. When the great-uncle died in 1892, Kathleen found herself incarcerated in an Anglican convent in Scarborough. Here the life of religious observance was so intolerably strict that she left an avowed agnostic; after undergoing an operation for appendicitis, from which she very nearly died, Kathleen was asked if she would like to see a priest. 'God forbid,' she murmured. So when her brother Rosslyn turned up wearing a dog-collar the nurses tried to get rid of him. 'It's all right,' Kathleen told them. 'He's my brother. I had forgotten he was a clergyman.'[14]

Kathleen Bruce must have had a remarkable strength of character to have survived relatively unscathed such a disadvantaged childhood and adolescence. In the words of her son's biographer, she became in fact 'a woman of forceful personality, unconventional opinions and ready wit'.[15] She had also inherited, or otherwise acquired, very considerable gifts as a sculptor, entering the Slade School of Fine Art in 1900, when she was twenty-two. By the age of twenty-four she was living a thoroughly Bohemain life on the Left Bank in Paris, penniless but fulfilled. Her formative years could not have been in greater contrast to those of Robert Scott, the conventional naval officer. Kathleen knew the actor-manager Nigel Playfair and Picasso, Isadora Duncan and Gertrude Stein. But it was men who mattered most to her, and she entertained an *idée fixe*; if ever she married it would be to a man worthy to be the father of her son.

It never seriously occurred to her that her first-born might be a girl, although if it had been, the name reserved for the baby was Griselda.

Scott would not have wanted to be an explorer had he not possessed a streak of romanticism, even of otherworldliness, that cut across the attributes normally associated with service personnel (he was perfectly capable of forgetting a dinner engagement or of pouring milk over a plate of curry), and it would be a mistake to imagine he was entirely strait-laced. Outside his circle of naval friends, he could number the playwright J.M. Barrie, and, fortunately for his matrimonial prospects, Mabel Beardsley, sister of the 'decadent' homosexual artist Aubrey Beardsley. Mabel Beardsley was a friend also of Kathleen Bruce, and it was in December 1906 that Mabel Beardsley invited Scott and Kathleen Bruce to lunch. As no spark was ignited at the lunch party, in October 1907 Mabel had another shot at match-making, and invited Kathleen and Scott to a rarefied tea party, graced by two of her most distinguished friends, the novelist Henry James and the actor Ernest Thesiger.

Although probably not yet in love, a certainty that only dawned with the birth of her son, Kathleen decided that Scott was the man to father her child, which was a compliment if only because she had been chased by many suitors. As for Scott, he is said to have fallen 'headlong in love', but this may be doubted. The letters he wrote to Kathleen were more concerned with self-doubt and money than with his happiness; he had no sense of humour, and humourless people seldom surrender to love. He had continual nagging doubts about the marriage, almost as though he felt he was falling into a trap. His arguments against an engagement and marriage were peculiarly mercenary and dreary: he had no private income; he was still supporting his mother, which reduced his disposable income to £600 a year; he did not even have a house. It is not possible to date precisely the day on which Robert Scott and Kathleen Bruce agreed to marry, but their engagement seems to have been a very short one. J.M. Barrie only knew of it on 5 August 1908, and they were married a month later.

After inspecting a number of properties they could not possibly afford, Scott and Kathleen settled on No. 174 Buckingham Palace Road, a terraced house they took on a 27-year lease for £1 a week. It has long since been demolished to make room for a bus station. Although Scott admired, indeed was fascinated by, Kathleen's exuberance and free-wheeling spirit (she was amazingly emancipated for the times), he realized she would be unlikely to get along with his mother and prim and proper sisters. But she was a pragmatist, independent and single-minded, and seems to have had no qualms at all about coping without a man about the house while he was at sea, an attitude much to be commended in a sailor's wife. James Lees-Milne, who knew Kathleen well in later years and wrote her *Times* obituary when she died in 1947, thought her the worst dressed woman he knew, and considered her great failing was 'to blow the trumpets of her family' until one was deafened.[16]

Kathleen's aunt, Zoë Thomson, was the widow of William Thomson, Archbishop of York from 1862 until his death in 1890, and as a result, in 1900 she had been granted a grace and favour apartment in the Princesses Amelia and Caroline's lodgings at Hampton Court Palace.[17] (Amelia and Caroline were the second and third daughters respectively of George II.) Through her influence it was arranged that Kathleen should marry Scott in the chapel at Hampton Court, a Royal Peculiar and hence in the personal patronage of the king, whose consent to a member of the Royal Victorian Order being married there was readily obtained. Oddly enough, Scott dispensed with his naval uniform for the wedding, which took place on 2 September 1908, just a week after an announcement of the engagement had appeared in the *Tatler*.[18] He wore morning dress, and Kathleen splashed out on a wedding dress of white satin trimmed with lace.

Scott gave his address as HMS *Bulwark*, a ship he had joined as captain on 30 May, and Kathleen, rather grandly, for she could only have been lodging temporarily with her aunt, gave her's as Hampton Court

Palace. Her late father she described, quite correctly, as a clerk in holy orders, but Scott, presumably feeling that 'brewer' sounded demeaning, placated the shade of his father by describing him as 'A Gentleman'. The marriage entry was signed by Scott's mother, who in 1915 was herself assigned quarters at Hampton Court (as was Sir Ernest Shackleton's widow, in 1930), by Captain Henry Campbell, Scott's best man, and by Kathleen's brother Wilfred, who gave her away. The Reverend S.G. Ponsonby, rector of Stoke Damerel, the parish where Scott had been born, officiated.[19] The honeymoon was spent in France, at Etretat, a small fishing port with outstanding cliff scenery on the Normandy coast just north of Le Havre. On their return, Scott resumed his duties aboard *Bulwark*. (In semi-disgrace following his collision while in charge of *Albemarle* Scott had gone on half-pay in August 1907, and on 25 January 1908 had been downgraded with the captaincy of HMS *Essex*, a cruiser and a good deal less expensive to replace than a battleship should anything go amiss. It was from *Essex* that four months later, having performed his penance, Scott had transferred to *Bulwark*, with a ship's company of 750 under his command.)

Shackleton had found it hard to forgive Scott for ordering his return from the Antarctic in 1903 after he had developed scurvy, and had been determined to go back with an expedition of his own. His avowed intent was to reach the South Pole, and to put Scott's exploratory deeds in the shade. Moreover, he was planning to launch his drive on the South Pole from Scott's old winter headquarters. In reality, Shackleton had a perfect right to do as he pleased, but Sir Clements Markham was more than a little anxious that it should be his protégé Scott who should be first at the Pole, and so he sought to cause discontent by describing Shackleton as the black sheep of Scott's expedition. In the end there was a reasonably amicable meeting in London between Scott and Shackleton, the latter promising to land further east than McMurdo Sound, possibly on King Edward VII Land.

Many of the men Shackleton wanted to recruit for his expedition had previously been with Scott, and if they were ever to return to the hardships of the Antarctic they wished to go with Scott again. Nevertheless, Shackleton eventually managed to assemble a team, and with generous backing from a Clydebank ship owner, on 30 July 1907 he sailed from the East India Dock. It is clear that by the time of Scott's first meeting with Kathleen Bruce, the year before, he had already determined to return south as well, writing to the secretary of the Royal Geographical Society six months before Shackleton's departure to say, 'It will soon be on record that I want to go and only need funds'.[20]

In view of the brief marriage they were to enjoy it was fortunate that towards the end of 1908 Scott was offered his second staff job at the Admiralty, as naval assistant to the Second Sea Lord; hence he was able to live at home, and it was probably in December of that year that his son was conceived.[21]

Scott launched his appeal for funds on 13 September 1909, Shackleton having returned to London on 14 June that year, hailed as a hero and shortly to be knighted, but having failed by 97 miles to reach the Pole. The next day, 14 September, at their home in Buckingham Palace Road, Kathleen gave birth to a son. Scott asked J.M. Barrie to stand as godfather, and the child was baptised Peter in honour of Peter Pan, who had first fluttered across the stage in 1904. Sir Clements Markham was the other godfather, although at seventy-nine perhaps rather aged for the task.

Scott was now so totally committed to returning south that in order to devote all his energy to fund-raising, on 2 December 1909 he resigned from his job at the Admiralty, remaining on half-pay, and transferring for administrative purposes, as he had when relieved of naval duties in 1901, to HMS *President*. He had already decided which ship to take, *Terra Nova*, and had managed to scrape up a deposit of £5,000 against the £12,500 being asked for her. He followed up his initial appeal, for £40,000, by addressing largely disinterested meetings in dreary industrial towns, spurred on by Kathleen, who had actually written to Scott before their marriage to say, 'Write and tell me that you *shall* go to the Pole. Oh dear what's the use of having energy and enterprise if a little thing like *that* can't be done. It's got to be done, so hurry up and don't leave a stone unturned.'[22]

Although acquiring funds was an onerous task, finding men enthusiastic to join the adventure was not so hard; by the end of Scott's recruitment drive an astonishing 6,000 men had volunteered to go to the South Pole with him.[23] The first to volunteer was the former navigator of the relief ship *Morning*, Lieutenant Edward Evans. He was twenty-six, and Scott appointed him second-in-command, ditching an officer who had sailed with him previously, Reginald Skelton, because Evans was prepared to put up £1,000. Someone else who purchased his place aboard, as assistant zoologist, was Apsley Cherry-Garrard; a cousin of Scott's publisher, he too came up with £1,000. Interviews took place in an office at No. 36 Victoria Street, and Kathleen, now the driving force behind Scott, was present at all of them. One of those Kathleen persuaded her husband to take on was an Indian Marine lieutenant, Henry Bowers, 'a tiny man, with no legs to speak of'. His references were so good and 'he himself so ugly and unprepossessing' that Kathleen thought 'A man with such physical disabilities and yet such testimonials must be first-rate at the job'.[24] Which he was. Bowers hero-worshipped Scott, and became an indispensable member of his second expedition.

'The main object of the expedition is to reach the South Pole,' Scott had announced when he opened his appeal, 'and to secure for the British Empire the honour of that achievement.'[25] 'A mere bagatelle' was how the *Pall Mall Gazette* described the £40,000 required, but many people murmured that any spare cash waiting to be collected should be diverted to more urgent use, like the alleviation of poverty.

As a large part of Scott's ambition was to set an example to future generations, it must have pleased him that many of those who rallied most enthusiastically to raise funds for equipment were school children. Forty-seven boys' and girls' schools held a whip-round to pay for dogs. They included well-known public schools like Beaumont College, Christ's Hospital and Felsted, grammar schools from across the country, and even the Regent Street Polytechnic. Although the dogs cost relatively little to purchase, their transportation, from Siberia to Vladivostok and then by steamer to Sydney in Australia and eventually to New Zealand, was a costly operation. The dogs were given names in Russian and English, together with nicknames, some of which – Jackass, Poodle, Wild One, One Eye – could not have inspired the expedition with too much confidence.

Robert Falcon Scott in captain's full dress uniform and wearing round his neck the collar and badge of the CVO, bestowed on him in 1904 by Edward VII. (Royal Geographical Society, London)

Scott and his wife, Kathleen, together for the last time, on board the *Terra Nova* shortly before she sailed from New Zealand at the start of Scott's second Antarctic expedition. (Popperfoto)

Slow progress by the *Terra Nova* through pack ice was a constant source of worry on the journey from New Zealand to the Antarctic. (Popperfoto)

The *Terra Nova* at Port Chalmers, New Zealand, on 29 November 1910, the day she sailed for the Antarctic. (Popperfoto)

'A day of disaster', Scott recorded on 8 January 1911, shortly after one of his three motor sledges had been hoisted ashore only to sink through the ice. (Popperfoto)

Scott leads one of the ponies ashore after making land at Cape Evans on 2 January 1911. The ponies endured a terrible journey and none survived the expedition. (Popperfoto)

Said to have been Scott's greatest friend, Edward Wilson, a doctor, zoologist and painter, accompanied him on both Antarctic expeditions and died with Scott and Henry Bowers only 11 miles from safety. (Popperfoto)

Christmas Day 1910 was celebrated on board the *Terra Nova* in traditional festive style.
(Popperfoto)

After enduring 'the worst journey in the world' to secure specimen eggs of the Emperor
penguin, the two exhausted zoologists, Edward Wilson, left, and Apsley Cherry-
Garrard, right, enjoy a hot meal in the company of the intrepid Henry Bowers.
(Popperfoto)

Scott writes up his journal in the crowded hut that served as a base camp. (Popperfoto)

Living and sleeping accommodation in the base hut was cramped, to say the least. From bottom left, clockwise: Apsley Cherry-Garrard, assistant zoologist, Lieutenant Henry Bowers, Captain Lawrence Oates, Cecil Meares, in charge of the dogs, and Edward Atkinson, a Royal Naval surgeon and parasitologist. (Popperfoto)

On 13 May 1911 the *Illustrated London News* reproduced a photograph of Scott about to set out on a depot-laying trek prior to his assault on the South Pole, which commenced on 1 November that year. (*Illustrated London News*)

Captain Lawrence Oates of the 6th Inniskilling Dragoons, chosen only at the last minute to make the final assault on the South Pole. His decision to walk out alone into a blizzard in a vain attempt to save the lives of his comrades has become a byword for heroism. (Popperfoto)

The cairn built to cover the bodies of Scott, Wilson and Bowers eight months after they were discovered dead, just 11 miles from One Ton Depot and their vital supplies. (Popperfoto)

SUCH A
MERRY CREW

The brief history of naval exploration in the Antarctic began with Captain Cook's crossing of the Antarctic Circle in 1773. In 1841 Captain James Ross of the Royal Navy fought his way through pack ice to enter what is now the Ross Sea, and it was on 28 January 1841 that the Great Ice Barrier first came into view. 'What was beyond it,' Captain Ross mused, 'we could not imagine.'[1] (It was, in fact, Scott's first Antarctic expedition that began to unfurl the facts.) It was not until 1874, when Scott was six, that the first steam vessel crossed the Antarctic Circle. Before the turn of the century, other nations – Norway and Belgium, for instance – were expressing interest in the area, which had long been a rich source of profit, gained at great danger from storm and ice, for whale hunters. Hence by the time of Scott's adventures Clements Markham was striving to bring pressure to bear on the government of the day to mount expeditions to ensure the survival of British sovereignty in the region.

Compared to the Arctic, where bears and foxes and over 1,000 species of plants may be encountered, the Antarctic has nothing to commend it. This barren wilderness, that permits the existence on the coast of a primitive lichen and a few mosses, extends over 5½ million square miles. It is almost entirely covered by an ice sheet 6,000 ft thick. Around the Pole itself the annual mean temperature is −65 degrees, while temperatures of −124 degrees have been recorded elsewhere. Ninety per cent of the world's snow and ice is located in the Antarctic; blizzards are frequent. In this godforsaken place only seals, whales and hardy penguins have any business to be.

Yet, in 1910, in the spirit of schoolboy adventure, there took place a mad scramble to go there. One of those who thought it would be 'a wheeze' – he believed the Antarctic was 'very healthy, although inclined to be cold' – was an Old Etonian, Lawrence Edward Grace Oates, a captain in the 6th Inniskilling Dragoons. He had been wounded and mentioned in dispatches during the Boer War, rode to hounds, and had no difficulty waving a cheque for £1,000 to secure a berth on the *Terra Nova*. His value to Scott was meant to be his knowledge of horseflesh, yet someone wholly ignorant about horses, Cecil Meares, who was supposed to be buying dogs in Manchuria, was empowered to choose the horses as well. Almost without exception the animals he purchased were decrepit.

Edward Wilson was eager to go a second time, with a meteorologist, three geologists, a biologist and a physicist as colleagues. Two surgeons were included in the crew, together with a Royal Navy lieutenant called Victor Campbell, known as the wicked mate. In all, there was a ship's complement of sixty-five; seven officers, a scientific staff of a dozen, and thirty-two men known as the ship's party – able seamen, firemen, a shipwright and so on. From Russia, Scott recruited a dog driver by the name of Demetri Gerof and a groom called Anton Omelchenko. One of the last crew members to be signed on was Scott's brother-in-law, Wilfrid Bruce, a lieutenant in the Royal Naval Reserve. Among the seven petty officers was Edgar Evans, desperate to join a second expedition, from which he would not return.

Ernest Shackleton had discovered 'the terrible Beardmore Glacier' beyond which lay the South Pole, and Scott told Norwegian reporters that the 120 mile climb he planned to make over the glacier would be 'the nut that will be the hardest to crack'.[2] He and Kathleen were in Norway, on a hurried excursion to test newly invented motor sledges in conditions that bore little resemblance to the Antarctic, and it was during this brief visit that he recruited a ski expert, Tryggve Gran, who, like several of the expedition members, was to keep and publish a diary. Born in 1889, Gran was only twenty-one when *Terra Nova* sailed and was the youngest man aboard. To become anything like an expert skier takes years of training and practice, yet Gran was expected to pass on his skills to the other men on arrival in the Antarctic.

But everything was rushed, and many corners were cut. In fact, Scott spent just nine months in preparation for his voyage, because he felt that time was fast running out. Every day, it seemed, came news of rival expeditions about to set out: American, Scots, German, Japanese.

The ship Scott was fitting out, *Terra Nova*, had seen twenty-six years service as a whaler – 'an absolute wreck, fit only for the knacker's yard' in the opinion of one perhaps rather fastidious shipwright.[3] Scott's own outlook, surprisingly and possibly over-optimistic, can be gauged from his account of the workmanship carried out. A leak was discovered, and after repairs had been effected he noted in his journal, 'The ship still leaks, but the amount of water entering is little more than one would expect in an old wooden vessel'.[4]

Stalls for fifteen ponies were incorporated, although horses were totally unfit for life in the Antarctic, requiring every scrap of food to be transported from England. A good deal of space normally reserved for the crew was also commandeered for the stowing of sledges and scientific equipment, and more valuable space was taken up by the three almost entirely useless motor sledges. Into an expensive ice house were crammed

3 tons of ice, 162 carcases of mutton and 3 of beef, together with sweetbreads and kidneys. Four hundred and sixty-two tons of coal were heaved aboard, 30 tons coming to rest on the upper deck. Scott noted:

> The sacks containing this last, added to the goods already mentioned, make a really heavy deck cargo, and one is naturally anxious concerning it; but everything that can be done by lashing and securing has been done.

He added: 'The appearance of confusion on deck is completed by our thirty-three dogs chained to stanchions and bolts on the main hatch between the motor sledges.'[5]

Scott was anxious to leave New Zealand towards the end of November because he believed a large ship like the *Terra Nova* (700 tons gross) would be able to cut through the pack ice expected at that time of year, thus enabling the expedition to reach the South Pole – he had planned the precise day – on 22 December 1911, the day the sun would achieve its maximum altitude. Hence *Terra Nova* was scheduled to sail for New Zealand on 1 June 1910. But first Scott was invited by Queen Alexandra, widowed since 6 May, to call at Buckingham Palace, where she presented him with two Union Jacks, one to remain at the furthest southern point Scott was able to reach; the other, for some peculiar reason, she requested to fly there for a while and then be returned to her. Equally anxious to offer a helping hand, the new king, George V, gave Scott a portrait of himself to hang in the wardroom.

Having waved *Terra Nova* off, Scott and his wife said goodbye to their baby son on 16 July, and departed from Southampton for Cape Town in the steamer *Saxon*. Even now there was a shortfall of £8,000. This was a cause of far greater concern than the news they received on their arrival in South Africa, that an experienced Norwegian explorer called Captain Roald Amundsen was planning an expedition to discover more about the Arctic. The Arctic, after all, was in the north. Scott was going south. But while in the middle of a dispiriting fund-raising tour of the Cape, Scott heard the news that Amundsen had changed tack and was on some sort of secret mission heading south. Confirmation of his worst fears was received when Scott arrived at Melbourne. Awaiting him was a telegram from Amundsen. It read: 'Beg Leave Inform You Proceeding Antarctic.'

So now the race was on. No matter how often Scott was to protest that an important part of his mission was to gather more scientific information, his stated objective for a long time had been to gain for the British Empire the honour of planting the Union Jack at the South Pole before anyone else. But for Scott the Pole was a personal objective as well: succeed, and he would have entered the coming European conflict as an admiral and a KCB; fail, and his naval career would most probably have shuddered to a halt. Whether the knowledge that there was now for certain a tough and very competent competitor in the field depressed him, so that at times his judgement failed, or spurred him and his companions to superhuman efforts, is a matter for conjecture. In all probability, it was six of one and half a dozen of the other.

There was another factor that urged Scott on to the South Pole; it was a do or die desire to outshine the distance covered by another, unacknowledged, rival, Ernest Shackleton.

Scott certainly did not hide the enormity of his task. 'No one can foretell our luck,' he said in public shortly before the expedition finally got under way:

> We may get through, we may not. We may have accident to some of the transports, to the sledges or to the animals. We may lose our lives. We may be wiped out. It is all a question that lies with providence and luck.[6]

This was stirring stuff but better left unsaid. Neither Amundsen nor Shackleton placed their companions' lives and their own reputations in the hands of providence or luck; they planned meticulously and took account of well-documented previous experience, relating in particular to the terrain (to which the hoofs of horses were hopelessly unsuited), the weather to be expected, and even the proper goggles to wear to prevent snow blindness. No remark was ever to play more tellingly into the hands of Scott's detractors; one can hardly imagine a confident general before a battle telling the world his side might all be wiped out. Certainly they would require an element of luck, and in the event it can, with some justification, be said they were unlucky. But unfortunately the whole expedition had been founded upon a blind, and very British, belief in the moral superiority of human muscle power over any other mode of transport, of virtue in suffering for its own sake – British because in its origins it was essentially puritanical. Rather than rely on professionally driven teams of dogs to get them to the Pole, Scott thought it far more manly for men to haul the sledges themselves. Five of them died as a result.

But that calamity lay in the future. At 2.57 p.m. on 26 November 1910, three minutes ahead of schedule, the *Terra Nova* 'pushed off' from the jetty at Lyttelton, whence *Discovery* had sailed in 1901. 'A great mass of people' had assembled, according to Scott, who with his wife had opted to have lunch on board a ship belonging to the New Zealand Company. Then they joined the crew of the *Terra Nova*, but 'left her inside the Heads', returning to the shore in a harbour tug. Scott then went for a stroll and managed to spot his ship disappearing into the distance, 'a little dot to the S E'.[7]

Two days later Scott and Kathleen caught a train to Port Chalmers, further south along the coast; it was

here that Scott planned to rejoin *Terra Nova*. On arrival
he found 'all well', and after paying a courtesy call on
the mayor he repaired to the wharf, where in bright
sunshine he encountered a 'very gay scene'.[8] It was 2.30
p.m. on 29 November when the *Terra Nova* finally set sail
from New Zealand, still with Kathleen Scott, Mrs
Wilson and Mrs Edward Evans, the wives of two other
members of the crew, on board. Once arrived at the
Heads, however, the ladies said goodbye and
disembarked in another harbour tug. Neither Mrs Scott
nor Mrs Wilson were to see their husbands again.

Scott's *Terra Nova* had only been at sea a day when he
reported the ship pitching in a south-westerly swell. 'All
in good spirits,' he added, 'except one or two sick.' One
of them may well have been himself. Like many a sturdy
naval officer before him – including Nelson himself –
Scott was often prone to seasickness, just as he was
likely to faint at the sight of blood. But those who
suffered most from the 'swaying, swaying continually to
the plunging, irregular motion' were the ponies. 'It
seems', Scott wrote, 'a terrible ordeal for these poor
beasts to stand this day after day for weeks together.' Yet
Scott had known that he was to sail one of the stormiest
seas in the world. Had he not considered how horses
would withstand such a journey before he took them?
He comforted himself with the thought that
'anatomically they possess a ligament in each leg which
takes their weight without strain'. The dogs, inevitably

tethered for the duration of the journey, did not fare much better. 'Occasionally', Scott tells us, 'some poor beast' emitted a long, pathetic whine.[9]

A portent of how the whole mad escapade might be going to end was penned by Scott on 2 December, only three days after the *Terra Nova* had left the safety of terra firma. 'A day of great disaster' his journal entry began. A gale blew up and cases of petrol and forage on the upper deck began to break loose. While grappling with the shifting cargo, the crew at times had to 'cling for dear life to some fixture to prevent themselves being washed overboard, and with coal bags and loose cases washing about, there was every risk of such hold being torn away'. Towards the end of a truly terrifying night Scott was informed that the pumps in the engine room had choked and water was rising over the gratings. This was the second ship Scott had taken to the Antarctic knowing quite well it was liable to leak.

With so much cargo on board there was little leeway for water, and by this time the ship was in danger of sinking. 'The scene on deck was devastating,' Scott recorded, 'and in the engine room the water, though really not great in quantity, rushed over the floor plates and frames in a fashion that gave it a fearful significance.'

For a night and a day, supervised by the tireless Lieutenant Evans, whom the men later cheered as their saviour, the crew simply bailed out the ship with buckets, the men singing sea shanties as they worked.

Two ponies died, a dog was drowned, and another pony was washed overboard and by the next wave washed back again. Yet by the end of this nightmare Scott found the ship sailing within two points of its course. He was making for the Ross Sea, for he knew that December was usually a fine month there, and because of the terrible conditions the animals were having to endure he was anxious to arrive within the Antarctic Circle without encountering another storm.

A week out, and he recorded everyone very cheerful. 'One hears laughter and song all day − it's delightful to be with such a merry crew.' That night, 7 December, they spotted their first iceberg. The next day, whales were seen.

By 11 December, a Sunday, the *Terra Nova* had encountered pack ice. 'I read Service in the wardroom,' Scott recorded. 'This afternoon all hands have been away on ski over the floes. It is delightful to get the exercise.'[10] The pack ice gave way, and they were able to sail on. Then it closed in again, and the ship came to a halt. 'Truly,' Scott wrote on 12 December, 'the getting to our winter quarters is no light task; at first the gales and heavy seas, and now this continuous fight with the pack ice.'

Within twenty-four hours, Scott had decided to preserve his stock of coal and to cease striving to cut through the ice. It must have been an anxious time, but while they waited for release from the ice they enjoyed ski instruction from the Norwegian sub-lieutenant Tryggve Gran, and it became so hot that one of the surgeons and the Soldier, as they had nicknamed Captain Oates, ended up stripped to the waist.[11]

By 16 December they were on their way again, but on the evening of 18 December Scott was moaning:

> What an exasperating game this is! – one cannot tell what is going to happen in the next half or even quarter of an hour. At one moment everything looks flourishing, the next day one begins to doubt if it is possible to get through.

And by the following day Scott was lamenting his bad luck – a lament that would eventually become his motif for the whole operation:

> On the whole, in spite of many bumps, we made good progress during the night, but the morning (present) outlook is the worst we've had. We seem to be in the midst of a terribly heavy screwed pack; it stretches in all directions as far as the eye can see, and the prospects are alarming from all points of view. I have decided to push west – anything to get out of these terribly heavy floes. Great patience is the only panacea for our ill case. It is bad luck.

He said he was afraid the rudder had been strained; it was stiff in one direction. 'We are in difficult circumstances altogether. This morning we have brilliant sunshine and no wind.'

By 20 December Scott was very seriously worried about his stocks of coal. 'We are making terrible inroads on our supply – we have come 240 miles since we first entered the pack streams.' During that night they drifted towards two large icebergs, 'and about breakfast time we were becoming uncomfortably close to one of them – the big floes were binding down on one another, but there seemed to be open water to the S.E., if we could work out in that direction.' It was constantly being at the mercy of ice, one minute permitting a way straight through, the next forcing Scott to change direction, that made his task of finding a suitable landing from which to establish winter quarters so frustrating.

By 22 December there was 'not a vestige of swell'. Scott thought 'Fortune has determined to put every difficulty in our path. We have less than 300 tons of coal left in a ship that simply eats coal. It's alarming – and then there are the ponies going steadily down hill in condition.' But their time was not entirely wasted drifting around; the parasitologist, Edward Atkinson, opened up a penguin and discovered a new tapeworm.

One exasperation followed another. On Christmas Eve they were caught up 'in a solid sheet of pack extending in all directions, save that from which we had come'. Scott was constantly called on to decide whether to let the boiler room fires die out when becalmed, knowing that it would take two tons of coal to start them up again:

> But this 2 tons would only cover a day under banked fires, so that for anything longer than twenty-four hours it is economy to put the fires out. At each stoppage one is called upon to decide whether it is to be for more or less than twenty-four hours.

It fell within the routine remit of a captain to read services on board ship, and in Scott's own case it did not indicate any great relish for religion. On Christmas Day he noted, not surprisingly, a full attendance at morning service 'and a lusty singing of hymns'. In the evening the officers enjoyed 'an excellent dinner', consisting of tomato soup, penguin breast 'stewed as an entrée', roast beef, plum pudding and mince pies, asparagus, champagne, port and liqueurs. The men 'had dinner at midday – much the same fare, but with beer and some whisky to drink. They seem to have enjoyed themselves much. Evidently the men's deck contains a very merry band.' It would have been unthinkable, in 1910, for the men and officers to eat together, even on Christmas Day while cooped up on board and striving to reach the bleakest place on earth. For Scott, a naval captain, the maintenance of class barriers under all circumstances was thought a cornerstone of good discipline, and he tended to fuss unbearably over trivial details. Unlike many of the officers who served under him, he had in any case as little rapport with the crew as he had with the dogs.

The festive menu was consumed only just in time. Two days later, largely because of poor ventilation in the ice house, it was found that a good deal of the meat had gone off, and carcases were duly hung in the rigging. Scott closed the volume of his journal he had now filled up 'under circumstances which cannot be considered cheerful'.

He was later to write home, 'The New Year's Eve found us in the Ross Sea, but not at the end of our misfortunes'.[12] And in his journal entry for 31 December he noted, 'We had a horrible night'. But as the clouds lifted to the west 'a splendid view of the great mountains was obtained'. At last they had sighted the land they would have to cross if they were to reach the South Pole.

F I V E

'WE OUGHT TO GET THROUGH'

Captain Scott's original plan, to land at Cape Crozier, was abandoned because of rough seas. Eventually they made fast, on 2 January 1911, at a point previously known as The Skuary, now renamed Cape Evans, 'in honour of our excellent second-in-command'.

'A day of disaster,' Scott wrote in his journal six days later. He had given orders, 'stupidly', as he was the first to admit, for the third and largest of the motor sledges to be unloaded without the ice being properly tested; the ice gave way and the sledge nose dived to the bottom of the sea.[1] Part of the trouble had been Scott's desire to disembark quickly, for he wanted the *Terra Nova* ready to sail as soon as possible with a party ordered to set up camp on King Edward VII Land.

Better results were achieved with the erection of a hut, divided, as Scott's naval training would have dictated instinctively, into separate quarters for the officers and men. It had always made sense for Clements Markham to insist that a sailor should navigate polar expeditions; whether it was such a good idea for an officer like Scott, so bent on tradition, to lead one once ashore remains a very open question. The hut measured 50 ft by 25 ft, stood 9 ft high, and by 18 January it had become a warm and convivial home from home, largely thanks to the initiative of Lieutenant Bowers, who every day 'conceives or carries out some plan to benefit the camp'. Bowers was to prove one of the most imaginative and heroic of the South Pole party.

Scott's overall strategy was to lay supply depots until almost the last moment, depend for transport on a combination of men, dogs, ponies and motor sledges, and rely on back-up by support parties. Unfortunately, he appeared to be incapable of holding a planning conference, sharing ideas or listening to criticism, so not everyone knew what was going on. A party left to lay supply depots on 24 January. The first depot they called Safety Camp, for it was considered sufficiently far inland to be free from the danger of ice breaking away. Those who left the hut with Scott, accompanied by eight ponies and all the dogs, were Edward Evans, Bowers, Captain Oates (who wrote to his mother to say he disliked Scott intensely 'and would chuck the thing if it was not that we are the British expedition and must beat the Norwegians'),[2] Atkinson, Cherry-Garrard, and Gran, three able seamen, and the Russian dog-driver, Demetri Gerof; his presence was essential because the dogs only understood words of command in Russian.

Already by the time the first depot was laid the ponies were causing concern, partly because all but one set of their snow-shoes had been left at Cape Evans; Oates, in charge of the ponies, had no faith in them. The snow was softer than expected, and instead of treading merrily along on firm ground the ponies floundered.

Two men had to be left behind at this point; Atkinson, who had a sore heel, and Petty Officer Thomas Crean, to keep him company. Equipped with provisions for five weeks, the depot-laying party set out again. Oates, who could be pig-headed as well as independently minded when he felt like it, deliberately left one pair of snow-shoes behind and Tryggve Gran was sent back for them on his speedy skis.

With the daytime sun softening the snow, Scott decided on night marches when the ground would be firmer, and they began to average 10 or 11 miles a night. But at Corner Camp they encountered their first blizzard, and were delayed for three days. When they were able to start off again they marched due south for ten nights to lay their final depot. By now three ponies were in very poor shape and Scott decided to send them home, ploughing on with only five. During the next forty-eight hours conditions grew steadily worse. It was colder than Scott had anticipated, the surface was bad, and heavy snowdrifts impeded the ponies. The dogs, by contrast, seemed to be enjoying themselves, and by now Scott may have been wondering why on earth he had not taken account of Shackleton's experience; he had set out with nineteen ponies, not one of which survived. Yet Scott had been well aware of the arguments in favour of dogs. They could draw about 100 lb while consuming half as much food as a man, and as dogs sweat through their paws their fur is unaffected by the cold, whereas in the morning the ponies were covered in ice.

Lunching with James Lees-Milne in November 1944, Scott's widow told him that her husband hated any unkindness to animals, that it was 'torture to him when they suffered on his account'.[3] Such sentiments may have accounted for Scott's idealistic, some would say masochistic, dream of dispensing with animals altogether. He once pronounced:

> No journey ever made with dogs can approach the height of that fine conception which is realised when a party of men go forth to face hardships, dangers and difficulties with their own unaided efforts, and by days and weeks of hard physical labour succeed in solving some great problem of the great unknown. Surely in this case the conquest is more nobly and splendidly won.[4]

Scott had an opportunity of putting his muscular Christian theories to the test when the five members of the expedition to make the final assault on the South Pole did so by dragging their own sledges, but without dogs in the initial stages they would have got nowhere at all. As for reliance on ponies, Scott had certainly made a bad miscalculation, entirely at odds with the mode of transport favoured by Amundsen, who was relying exclusively on dogs.

After struggling through temperatures of −21 degrees, advancing less than 7 miles one day, they deposited more than a ton of stores 142 miles from the Cape Evans hut. This they named One Ton Depot, the depot Scott and his companions so nearly reached on their return journey, but they had been laying down too few depots too far apart. Already signs were ominous. Oates's nose was frostbitten, as were Bowers's ears, and Meares had a bad toe.

As though the march to the Pole was not to prove dramatic enough, events took place before the final departure from the hut at the end of the year that would have finished off all but the most resolute, animals as well as men. One of the dogs, Stareek, broke loose and vanished, only to reappear eighteen days later, having followed the men's tracks for 200 miles without a meal. Within 12 miles of Safety Camp all the dogs vanished — down a crevasse. Only by the superhuman efforts of Scott, Wilson, Meares and Cherry-Garrard, aided by one particularly powerful brute called Osman, who was nearly choked by the trace round his collar, were the sledge and all but two dogs retrieved; the remaining two had slipped their harness and fallen a further 40 ft on to a snow ledge. Scott insisted on being lowered 65 ft to rescue them.

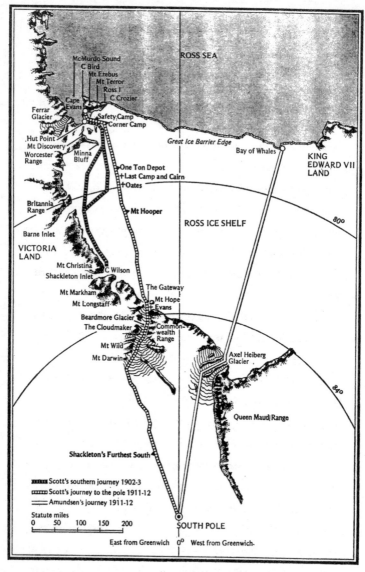

ROSS SEA

McMurdo Sound
C Bird
Mt Erebus
Mt Terror
Ross I
C. Crozier
Cape
Evans
Ferrar
Glacier
Safety Camp
Corner Camp

Great Ice Barrier Edge

Bay of Whales

KING
EDWARD VII
LAND

Hut Point
Mt Discovery
Worcester
Range
Minna
Bluff

One Ton Depot
+Last Camp and Cairn
+Oates

Britannia
Range

Mt Hooper

ROSS ICE SHELF

800

Barne Inlet

VICTORIA
LAND

Mt Christina   C Wilson
Shackleton Inlet

The Gateway
Mt Hope
Evans

Mt Markham
Mt Longstaff
Beardmore Glacier
The Cloudmaker
Common-
wealth
Range

Axel Heiberg
Glacier

Mt Wild
Mt Darwin

Queen Maud Range

840

Shackleton's Furthest South

Scott's southern journey 1902-3
Scott's journey to the pole 1911-12
Amundsen's journey 1911-12
Statute miles
0   50   100   150   200

SOUTH POLE

East from Greenwich   0°   West from Greenwich.

Routes to the South Pole. (From Huxley, *Scott of the Antarctic*, Weidenfeld &
Nicolson)

Back at Safety Camp, Scott found a letter from Victor Campbell, in charge of the *Terra Nova*, telling him they had been unable to disembark on Edward VII Land and had returned to the Bay of Whales, where they had encountered Amundsen. Cautious courtesies had been exchanged and the Norwegian was entertained to lunch aboard the *Terra Nova*, during which it was learned that he had with him a team of 116 dogs, and was not planning to sledge to the South Pole before the next Antarctic summer. The Bay of Whales was some 60 miles closer to the South Pole than McMurdo Sound, and Amundsen said he thought that Shackleton would have got to the Pole had he made his base at the Bay of Whales.

Having digested the facts, Scott decided to stick to his timetable and 'go forwards and do our best for the honour of the country without fear or panic'.[5]

Meanwhile Scott needed to get everyone back to the hut, but sent only Bowers, Crean and Cherry-Garrard ahead with four surviving ponies and the loaded sledges; Scott himself, with Oates and Gran, stayed with a pony that had collapsed and was clearly dying. It might have been more sensible and humane to have shot it. That evening Bowers made camp on a snow-covered stretch of ice he deemed to be safe; his ponies could go no further anyway. He awoke in the night to find the ice had cracked and his camp was on a drifting floe. Displaying immense heroism, Bowers stayed with the three ponies still alive, and whenever two floes drifted close enough he, Crean and Cherry-Garrard hauled the sledges across and tried to induce the ponies to jump, terrified as they were by the appearance of killer whales.

It was six hours before the stranded party reached the Barrier's edge, when Crean volunteered to take a note to Scott by attempting to negotiate broken ice patrolled by hungry whales, and then a 20 ft cliff. This he somehow managed to do – one slip would have been fatal – and when Scott and Oates arrived on the scene they contrived to manufacture a ladder out of sledges and then to dig a ramp for the ponies to climb. But before they could move the poor creatures, the ice moved. In the morning the animals were still alive, having drifted against a spur jutting out from the Barrier. Bowers and Oates made their way across the floes and reached them, but one of the ponies fell into the water. Oates was armed with a pick-axe, and used it to dispatch the struggling beast. Scott managed to haul one pony up the Barrier edge, but before they could rescue the third animal Wilson, who had come to help, fell in, at which moment a part of the Barrier broke away. With killer whales on the look-out for a meal, Scott ordered all the men up, and Bowers grabbed a pick-axe and mercifully slew the remaining stranded animal. Scott had begun his journey to lay depots with eight ponies. He got back to the hut with two.

By now the members of the expedition were hardened by bitter experience. 'Fortune is not being very kind to us,' Scott had good cause to write. But an even worse experience was in store for Wilson, Cherry-Garrard and Bowers. Although by mid-April Scott had announced that the sledging season was over, Wilson conceived the almost lunatic ambition, while he happened to be in the right part of the world, to procure specimen eggs of the Emperor penguin.

Wilson had reason to believe that the Emperor was the oldest and most primitive of any species of bird. To study its evolution he needed fertile eggs. These would be in the right stage of incubation in July. What could be more simple than to purloin a few while the male penguins, not over blessed with intelligence (they are quite liable to cradle a lump of ice instead of an egg), stood for two months at a stretch, usually in a blizzard and always without food, incubating a single egg, in permanent darkness and 100 degrees of frost?

Wilson's destination was Cape Crozier. He and Bowers both kept a diary, and fortunately for posterity, so did Cherry-Garrard. His account of the murderous adventure was published as *The Worst Journey in the World*, and has become a classic in the literature of exploration.[6] He, Wilson and Bowers left Cape Evans, where the expedition had reassembled in early April, on 27 June 1911. It was so cold they could not roll up their sleeping bags, and because of the cold it took them four hours each night to make camp. Progress was at the rate of about 5 miles a day. Hence it took them a fortnight to cover the 67 miles to the Cape.

They could never take off their gloves or their fingers would have frozen. Even the liquid in their blisters froze, and it was too cold to sleep. But eventually they reached the rookery – at the foot of a cliff, down which they had to scramble in the dark. They extracted five eggs, three of which were smashed on the way back up the cliff. That night a hurricane blew away their tent. After two nights in the open none of them expected to survive, but then somehow or other Bowers managed to locate the tent, and more dead than alive they staggered back to the hut. Wilson never lived to take his hard-won eggs to England, and they were deposited at the Natural History Museum by Cherry-Garrard, who was virtually ignored by the custodian and refused a receipt.

Scott was becoming increasingly worried about transport. He had lost four dogs during the winter, one having disappeared and three others dying for no apparent reason. 'I'm afraid we can place little reliance on our dog-teams,' he commented, 'and reflect ruefully on the misplaced confidence with which I regarded the provision of our transport.'[7]

On 6 June 1911, Scott's forty-third birthday was celebrated with champagne. Anniversaries were ritually recalled. Even while setting out in search of the penguin eggs, Bowers, the most courteous as well as courageous of men, remembered that during the course of the journey Wilson would have his thirty-ninth birthday, and thought to pack a tin of sweets as a present. Scott's age, so advanced compared to many of his team (Cherry-Garrard, for instance, was only twenty-five in 1911), is seldom commented on, but he was middle-aged and well past the age when most men would have considered undergoing the rigours of an expedition into the heart of the Antarctic landmass. However, it is a fact that on no occasion did he impede progress. On the contrary, in every particular the other men were expected to keep up with the pace he set, which was often far too strenuous. But idle hands and laziness in others he could not abide. He was intolerant of illness, and in trying to prove his own invincibility he often came near to breaking others.

While waiting for the off, fixed for 1 November, Scott undertook a gentle little hike of 175 miles for scientific purposes, he and three companions dragging 180 lb each for ten days without the aid of dogs. One of those companions was the indestructible Bowers, 'a positive wonder', as Scott noted. 'I never met such a sledge traveller.' By now there seemed little doubt that Bowers would be selected for the final march to the Pole. The selection of Wilson, too, was almost a foregone conclusion. Scott also early on decided to include Petty Officer Edgar Evans in the ill-fated party. In choosing these men, Scott was inadvertently signing their death warrants, but given half a chance almost every man on the expedition would have swapped places with them. Cherry-Garrard was particularly disappointed not to be picked.

Having made a false start on 8 September, when it was too cold even for his dogs, Amundsen eventually set off for the Pole on 20 October. One can imagine how it preyed on Scott's mind, not knowing precisely when his rival would depart. In the event, Amundsen stole a twelve day march on Scott. Before setting out himself, Scott wrote to his wife to say, 'I feel mentally and physically fit for the work'. But the letter also contains an enigma. He had apparently not always felt up to his responsibilities, and 'The root of the trouble was that I had lost confidence in myself'. Why, he did not explain, presumably because Kathleen would know what he was talking about. He also wrote – again, without any explanation – 'Had I been what I am now, many things would have been avoided'.[8]

Someone else who wrote home at this stage was Bowers, whose devotion to his mother was second only to his devotion to God. After that came Scott. 'I cannot say too much of Scott', he told Mrs Bowers, 'as a leader and an extraordinarily clever and far-seeing man. I am Captain Scott's man and shall stick to him right through. God knows what the result will be, but we will do all that man can do and leave the rest in His keeping which we all are, and shall remain.'[9]

Similar, although strictly speaking pagan, sentiments were echoed by Scott when he closed that part of his journal he intended leaving at the hut with the words, 'The future is in the lap of the gods. I can think of nothing left undone to deserve success.'[10]

So saying, at 11 o'clock on the night of 1 November Scott led out from the hut a team consisting of Wilson, Bowers, Oates, Atkinson, Cherry-Garrard, a physicist called Charles Wright and two petty officers in addition to Evans, Thomas Crean and Patrick Keohane. Each man led a pony. Each pony was harnessed to a sledge. The dogs, with Meares and Gerof, who would make far greater speed, were to follow and catch them up. From the hut to the Pole Scott and his friends had to traverse 766 geographical miles – 880 statute miles – entirely on foot. Then they would have to face the return journey.

Had Scott rememberd to pack every necessity? Pills in case of suicide; certainly. The Union Jacks given to him by Queen Alexandra; alas, no. Gran had to be summoned by field telephone to retrieve them on his skis.

The snow was soft. It should have been hard. The ponies again floundered. The average progress was barely 10 miles a day. After fifteen days they reached One Ton Depot, and had a twenty-four hour rest.

Oates had considered the ponies 'the most unsuitable scrap-heap crowd of unfit creatures that could possibly be got together', but despite their age they did rather well. However, it was not long before one of the ponies was shot, to provide food for the dogs. One by one, the others were shot. Bowers kept one of the pony's hoofs and marked the spot where he had secreted it, for he planned to collect it on the way back, a forlorn hope as it transpired. But nobody was seriously anticipating disaster. Oates had sent home for books to read during the course of the following winter to help him pass his examinations for promotion to major.

Every 70 miles or thereabouts a depot was laid for the returning parties. Scott maintained his journal – he was to do so until the very end – and in it he wrote, on 3 December, 'Our luck in weather is preposterous'. They were now marching in a snowstorm, so severe it nearly buried the sledges. Conditions were 'simply horrible'. On the morning of 5 December Scott wrote, 'One cannot see the next tent, let alone the land. What on earth does such weather mean at this time of year?'

Only a dozen miles from the dreaded Beardmore Glacier the expedition was halted by the weather for four vital days. 'A hopeless feeling descends on one,' Scott groaned, 'and is hard to fight off.' Had Scott not lost four days at the foot of the glacier he might have obtained One Ton Depot on the return march four days before the disastrous blizzard that ensured his death.

No one complained out loud. 'I did not expect nor desire a bed of roses,' Bowers was to write. 'Nor do I now, nor for worlds would I change my position with any other man on God's earth.'[11]

Like Bowers, Wilson was some kind of Christian pragmatist. Having fed his pony all his own biscuits he settled down to read Tennyson's *In Memoriam*, not in the least put out by the thought of death. 'All will be as it is meant to be.'[12]

When the blizzard died down they set off again, but the going was so soft the ponies could scarcely manage 5 or 6 yards at a time. In eleven hours they covered 5 miles. That night the five remaining ponies were shot. The depot they now laid was named, appropriately enough, Shambles Camp. 'Thank God the horses are all now done for and we begin the heavier work ourselves', were Wilson's stoic sentiments.[13]

Two days later the party reached the foot of the Beardmore, and Meares and Gerof set off for home with the dogs, carrying letters from those who were to continue. Scott wrote to Kathleen that things were not as rosy as they might be. Fortunately he did not know, although he may have guessed, that the Norwegians had already attained the 10,000 ft summit. And so they struggled on, each man hauling an appalling 200 lb in snow so soft they sank with every step. Those with snow blindness were in agony. Conditions were so bad that on 13 December they made just 4 miles in nine hours.

A week later, Scott was obliged to make a tough decision that his companions must all have been dreading; he ordered four of the party to make their way back to the hut. They were Atkinson, Wright,

Keohane and Cherry-Garrard, who thought Scott 'very put about' and was seriously wondering if Scott himself was fit enough to go on. 'Scott was fairly wound up,' Bowers wrote. To Kathleen, Scott dashed off a note to say, 'We are struggling on, considering all things, against odds'. Later that night, having made a stupendous effort to put fog and crevasses behind them, he added, 'We ought to get through'.[14]

With the first returning party on their way home, Cherry-Garrard having made a gift to Scott of tobacco as a Christmas present, the remaining men continued to climb for another exhausting sixteen days, now dragging a mere 190 lb per man. They had twelve weeks' supply of oil and food, some of which nearly ended at the bottom of a crevasse on Christmas Day, when the chief stoker almost fell to his death.

On Boxing Day they camped on the 86th parallel, and then began to make better progress, covering sometimes 17 miles in a day. But on New Year's Eve Petty Officer Evans cut his hand. The wound, superficially a fairly minor one, never healed, and may have contributed to his death. Two days later another misfortune occurred, an error of judgement on the part of Scott. He decided to take four men with him to the Pole instead of three, as originally envisaged. In addition to Wilson, Bowers and Petty Officer Evans, Scott now informed Oates that he too would be coming.

It is no disrespect to the memory of Captain Oates to

suggest that the reason Scott suddenly decided to include him in the final party was because he was an army officer, and in the romantic way such men as Scott sometimes think, he felt it appropriate that the Army should be represented at the Pole alongside the Navy and the world of science. But he had had months in which to ponder this. What taking five to the Pole instead of four meant was that essential tasks like cooking would take longer, and worse still, that rations so carefully weighed out in the depots would have to be reallocated, so that the men returning ahead of Scott would leave supplies for five, not four. It was one of the worst errors of judgement Scott ever made.

The three men told to return at this point were devastated, in particular Scott's loyal and efficient second-in-command, Lieutenant Evans. Lashly, the stoker, and Petty Officer Crean were in tears as they said goodbye. Scott and his remaining companions had a further 169 miles to go, and Scott expected to reach the Pole in about ten days. 'A last note from a hopeful position,' he wrote to Kathleen. 'I think it's going to be all right.'[15]

And indeed it did begin to look as if all the deprivation and hardship they had endured might in the end pay off. Although the surface remained bad they made fairly steady progress. 'What castles one builds', Scott wrote, 'now hopefully that the Pole is ours.'[16] But on 8 January 1912 they were held up for twenty-four hours by a blizzard, and Scott consoled himself that the rest would benefit Edgar Evans's injured hand. It did not. On 9 January they reached the point where Shackleton had turned back, and the hope must have been that they were further south than any other man before. But they were experiencing 50 degrees of frost at night, and Scott remained a worried man.

When they believed themselves to be only 97 miles from the Pole they made a depot of a week's provisions. They were all tiring now and the going remained very bad indeed. 'Another hard grind in the afternoon and five (geog.) miles added. About seventy-four miles from the Pole – can we keep this up for seven days?' Later: 'If we can do another four marches we ought to get through. It is going to be a close thing.'[17]

Scott's determination now was to reach the South Pole even if he was unable to return alive; all thought of turning back had long been given up, if indeed it had ever been entertained. But if Scott took a hard, realistic look at the physical condition of his party he must have wondered what their chances were of regaining the hut. Even before they had reached their objective they had worn out their bodies, and they were beginning to feel unaccountably cold, a sure sign that their vitality was draining away.

It was the weather that seemed to be their deter-mined enemy. Were it not for Bowers ('Bowers in my shadows directed me') Scott would have found it almost impossible to steer in the mist and overcast sky. And then the sun broke through – only to mock them. On 16 January Bowers saw something ahead which looked like a cairn. Eventually they came upon the remains of a camp, and in the snow a multitude of paw marks. They knew the Norwegians had beaten them.

Oates, Evans and Bowers all had frostbite. Bowers wrote to his mother to say that everything was fine, but who was supposed to deliver this letter remains a mystery. 'Great God! This is an awful place', was Scott's summing-up, a remark which has recently found its way into an anthology of scorn.[18]

On 17 January Scott wrote, 'We have had a horrible day – add to our disappointment a head wind 5 to 5, with a temperature –22 degrees'. The next morning he concluded they were 3½ miles from the Pole, 'one mile beyond it and 3 to the right'.[19] One and a half miles from the Pole, they calculated, they came upon another tent, occupied on 16 December by Amundsen and four others. Inside was a note addressed to Scott, asking him to forward a letter to King Haakon of Norway, brother-in-law of George V.

Bowers took photographs and Wilson sketched. They marched 7 miles south-south-east where they believed themselves to be within half a mile of the Pole, built a cairn, planted their Union Jacks, photographed themselves and set off for home. 'Good-bye to most of the day-dreams', Scott later wrote, as he braced himself for the 800 mile slog back to the hut.[20]

SIX

A SCENE OF WHIRLING DRIFT

I'm afraid the return journey is going to be dreadfully tiring and monotonous,' Captain Scott wrote in his journal on 19 January 1912. More worryingly, the following day he noted that Lawrence Oates was 'feeling the cold and fatigue more than most of us'.[1] By 22 January their ski boots were beginning to show signs of wear. In effect, men and equipment both were coming to the end of their useful lives.

On 23 January Scott recorded that they had come along 'at a great rate and should have got within an easy march of our depot had not Wilson suddenly discovered that Evans' nose was frostbitten – it was white and hard'. Evans was 'a good deal run down', with blisters on his fingers. 'He is very much annoyed with himself, which is not a good sign.' Scott thought that he, Wilson and Bowers were 'as fit as possible under the circumstances'. Oates, however, was still suffering from cold feet. Scott wrote:

One way and another, I shall be glad to get off the summit! We are only about 13 miles from our 'Degree and half' Depot and should get there tomorrow. The weather seems to be breaking up. Pray God we have something of a track to follow to the Three Degree Depot – once we pick that up we ought to be right.

But the next morning he was reporting 'Things beginning to look a little serious'. By lunch time a strong wind had developed into a blizzard, and they had been obliged to get into their sleeping bags. 'It was a bad march but we covered 7 miles.' He recorded 'the second full gale since we left the Pole', and added, 'I don't like the look of it'. *Was* the weather breaking up, he wondered? 'If so, God help us, with the tremendous summit journey and scant food. Wilson and Bowers are my standby. I don't like the easy way in which Oates and Evans get frostbite.'

They found their Half Degree Depot all right. But on 25 January Scott again noted now Oates was suffering from very cold feet, Evans's fingers and nose were in a bad state, and that night, Scott wrote, Wilson was 'suffering torture from his eyes'. Blizzards were their bugbear, 'not only stopping our marches, but the cold damp air takes it out of us'.

27 January: 'We are slowly getting more hungry.'

28 January: 'We are getting more hungry, there is no doubt.'

To add to their plight, on 30 January Wilson strained a tendon in his leg. 'It has given pain all day and is swollen to-night. Of course, he is full of pluck over it, but I don't like the idea of such an accident here.' That night, Evans lost two finger-nails. 'His hands are really bad,' Scott recorded, 'and to my surprise he shows signs of losing heart over it.' Fortunately Wilson's leg began to mend, but it seemed quite obvious that Edgar Evans was running down fast.

On 2 February it was Scott's turn to injure himself, coming 'an awful "purler"' on his shoulder. A worse incident was to occur two days later when Scott and Evans fell into a crevasse, Evans hitting his head in such a manner as eventually to prove fatal. It was his second fall, and Scott noticed he was becoming 'rather dull and incapable'. He had almost certainly suffered concussion, the cure for which would have been to lie quietly in a hospital bed.

It is astonishing that in spite of hunger, extreme cold and fatigue Wilson could still summon the energy to collect fossils, amounting to an additional burden of 35 lb in weight. These specimens eventually found their way to England and were regarded as the most important scientific finds of the entire expedition, containing as they did evidence about the age and history of the Antarctic. Scott has been castigated for allowing time and energy, both in such short supply, to be squandered picking up bits of heavy rock, but perhaps he saw no reason not to grant a dying man his last request; he almost certainly knew by this time that none of them had any serious chance of survival.

On 11 February the party encountered atrocious conditions under foot, conditions Scott described as 'the worst ice mess I have ever been in'. They lost time by losing their direction, and on several occasions fell into crevasses. That day they spent twelve hours on the march. 'It was very hard work,' Scott wrote that night, 'but we had grown desperate.'

Conditions were so bad the following day that Scott thought they were 'in a very critical situation'. But on 13 February they found their next depot. 'It was an immense relief, and we were soon in possession of our 3½ days' food. The relief to all is inexpressible.'

By this time Evans was quite incapable of helping to make camp, while Bowers as well as Wilson was being attacked by snow blindness.

16 February: 'Evans has nearly broken down in brain, we think. He is absolutely changed from his normal self-reliant self.'

17 February: 'A very terrible day.' Evans had seemed a little better first thing in the morning, but could not keep up with the others. They had to wait for him, but he dropped back again. When he failed to reappear they went in search of the poor fellow. Scott was the first to reach him and was shocked by his appearance, 'on his knees, with clothing disarranged, hands uncovered and frostbitten, and a wild look in his eyes'.

Evans said he thought he must have fainted, and according to Scott 'showed every sign of complete collapse'. They could not abandon him, and they could not take him with them. It was the ultimate nightmare scenario. By the time they had got Evans into the tent he was, according to Scott, 'quite comatose', and fortunately for all concerned, he died peacefully in the early hours. Scott wrote:

> It is a terrible thing to lose a companion in this way, but calm reflection shows that there could not have been a better ending to the terrible anxieties of the past week. Discussion of the situation at lunch yesterday shows us what a desperate pass we were in with a sick man on our hands at such a distance from home.

In his last hours, Scott found the energy to pen letters to assorted knights and baronets, but no note to the wife of his staunch and gallant Petty Officer, nor was any attempt made to identify the burial place. Edgar Evans lies somewhere at the foot of the Beardmore Glacier.

Some time on 18 February, the day of Evans's death, Scott and his three remaining companions reached Shambles Camp. They did not linger. Scott was becoming increasingly alarmed by the weather. On 21 February he wrote, 'We never won a march of 8½ miles with greater difficulty, but we can't go on like this'. The next day: 'There is little doubt we are in for a rotten critical time going home, and the lateness of the season may make it really serious.' Although they continued to locate supplies, they were short of fuel. It had evaporated. 'Found store in order except shortage oil – shall have to be *very* saving with fuel.'

'Poor Wilson has a fearful attack of snow blindness . . . . Wish we had more fuel.'

While in camp on 24 February Scott wrote:

A little despondent again. We had a really terrible surface this afternoon and only covered 4 miles . . . I don't know what to think, but the rapid closing of the season is ominous. . . . It is a race between the season and hard conditions and our fitness and good food.

But they were in no condition to race, and at the miserable rate of progress they were making it is astonishing they got as far as eventually they did.

27 February: 'Desperately cold last night.'

29 February (1912 was a leap year): 'Expected awful march and for first hour got it. Then things improved and we camped after 5½ hours marching close to launch camp – 22½. Next camp is our depot and it is exactly 13 miles. It ought not to take more than 1½ days; we pray for another fine one.'

But blessings were in short supply. By 2 March Scott was reporting a shortage of oil again, the fact that Oates now had frostbitten toes, and a fall in temperature during the night to –40 degrees. The surface was 'simply awful'. They only managed 5½ miles, and Scott considered they were 'in a *very* queer street since there is no doubt we cannot do the extra marches and feel the cold horribly'.

The next day, 3 March, the wind, and the conditions under foot, were so bad their progress, if such it can be called, was reduced to 1 mile per hour. 'God help us,' Scott wrote, 'we can't keep up this pulling, that is certain. Amongst ourselves we are unendingly cheerful, but what each man feels in his heart I can only guess.' Yet it never occurred to them to jettison their precious cargo of rocks.

4 March: 'Things looking *very* black indeed.'

5 March: 'Regret to say going from bad to worse.' Oates's feet were in 'a wretched condition. One swelled up tremendously last night and he is very lame this morning . . . poor Soldier nearly done. It is pathetic enough because we can do nothing for him; more hot food might do a little, but only a little, I fear. We none of us expected these terribly low temperatures, and of the rest of us, Wilson is feeling them most; mainly, I fear, from his self-sacrificing devotion in doctoring Oates's feet.'

By now there seems no doubt that Scott had finally given up any hope of getting home. 'We mean to see the game through with a proper spirit', were the proper manly words expected of a leader, written for proper manly folk at home one day to read.

By 6 March Oates was unable to pull, but was 'wonderfully plucky, as his feet must be giving him great pain'. Once again, those with any chance at all of survival were at the mercy of a very sick comrade. 'If we were all fit', Scott wrote, 'I should have hopes of getting through, but the poor Soldier has become a terrible hindrance, though he does his utmost and suffers much I fear.'

7 March: 'One of Oates's feet *very* bad this morning; he is wonderfully brave. We still talk of what we will do together at home.'

Wilson's feet began to cause concern too, and by this time the party were covering half the distances they should have been and using twice the amount of energy to achieve even that. By 10 March Oates was asking Wilson if he thought he had any chance of surviving. Wilson said he did not know, but it was obvious to Scott that Oates believed he had reached the end of the road. But Scott also doubted whether, even without Oates holding them up, he, Bowers and Wilson had any serious prospects. 'With great care we might have a dog's chance, but no more. The weather conditions are awful, and our gear gets steadily more icy and difficult to manage.'

The morning of 10 March had been quite calm, but the wind soon got up again, and after travelling half an hour Scott saw that none of them could go on battling against such conditions. So they were forced to call a halt, 'and are spending the rest of the day in a comfortless blizzard camp, wind quite foul'.

Next morning Scott thought Captain Oates 'very near the end', and instructed Wilson to distribute 'the means of ending our troubles' – which was opium. No doubt he was hoping Oates would take the hint. He thought 6 miles a day was the limit of their endurance. They had food for seven days and were about 55 miles from One Ton Camp. But 6 miles per day would mean only 42 miles covered before their supplies ran out 13 miles from the crucial depot, and that would mean two days marching with no food, a virtual impossibility considering the atrocious weather and their poor state of health.

That was how close the calculations were. 'I doubt if we can possibly do it,' Scott wrote on 12 March. 'The surface remains awful, the cold intense, and our physical condition running down. God help us!'

Two days later: 'No idea there would be temperatures like this at this time of year with such winds. Truly awful outside the tent.'

By the next time he opened his journal he had lost track of dates. He thought it was 17 March. 'Tragedy all along the line.' The previous day Oates had admitted he could not go on and asked the others to leave him in his sleeping bag. This of course they refused to do, so he struggled on for a few more miles, and went to bed that night hoping not to wake. When he did wake it was still blowing a blizzard. 'I am just going outside and may be some time' were his last imperishable words.

'We knew that poor Oates was walking to his death,' Scott recorded for posterity, 'but though we tried to dissuade him, we knew it was the act of a brave man and an English gentlemen. We all hope to meet the end with a similar spirit, and assuredly the end is not far.'

At midday the temperature was again –40 degrees. 'Though we constantly talk of fetching through I don't think any one of us believes it in his heart.'

But very slowly they moved on, leaving Oates in his snowbound resting place. In November 1912 a search was made for his body, but he has never been found. By 18 March Scott, Wilson and Bowers were 21 miles from One Ton Depot. Still the Antarctic wind tore at them. Within the past two days Scott himself had developed frostbite, and he knew that even if he got back alive his foot would have to be amputated.

The next day they only had 15½ miles to go – 'and ought to get there in three days'. But they only had food for two days and barely a day's supply of fuel. 'The weather', Scott explained, 'doesn't give us a chance.'

Just 11 miles from the depot they were again held up by a blizzard, and for the last time.

21 March: 'To-day forlorn hope, Wilson and Bowers going to depot for fuel.' But they never even set out.

Thursday, March 22 and 23: Blizzard bad as ever – Wilson and Bowers unable to start – to-morrow last chance – no fuel and only one or two of food left – must be near the end. Have decided it shall be natural – we shall march for the depot with or without our effects and die in our tracks.

Thursday, March 29. Since the 21st we have had a continuous gale from W.S.W. and S.W. We had fuel to make two cups of tea apiece and bare food for two days on the 20th. Every day we have been ready to start for our depot *11 miles* away, but outside the door of the tent it remains a scene of whirling drift. I do not think we can hope for any better things now. We shall stick it out to the end, but we are getting weaker, of course, and the end cannot be far.

It seems a pity, but I do not think I can write more . . .

For God's sake look after our people.

Eight months later the bodies of Scott, Wilson and Bowers were found. Wilson and Bowers were in their sleeping bags. Scott had his arm flung across Wilson.

The tent was collapsed to cover them, and a cairn built over their bodies. And there they remain to this day, frozen in the Antarctic waste.

No biography of Robert Falcon Scott should ever be attempted without due tribute being paid to those who endured so much with him and whose names are inseparable from his. Their memorial at Observation Hill, overlooking the Great Ice Barrier, carries words by Tennyson suggested by Apsley Cherry-Garrard: 'To strive, to seek, to find, and not to yield.'

E N V O I

For nearly a century there has been no need ever to refer to Captain Robert Scott, for there has always only been one Captain Scott – Scott of the Antarctic. His *Terra Nova* expedition ended up with debts of nearly £30,000. A Scott Memorial Fund was opened, to which King George and Queen Mary saw fit to contribute £100 each. After J.M. Barrie had written to *The Times* urging support, a total of £75,509 was eventually raised, out of which debts were paid off, £12,000 was set aside to establish the Scott Polar Research Institute in Cambridge, and modest grants (as little as £1,250 to the widow of Petty Officer Evans, who was expected to support herself and three children on a naval pension of £48 a year) were made to dependants. Scott's widow received £8,500 in trust for her son, and Peter received a further £3,500 in trust to pay for his education. He was sent to Oundle.

Living in the shadow of his father's name and fame, as Peter Scott was bound to do, his achievements would not have disappointed Robert Scott. He was appointed a Member of the Most Excellent Order of the British Empire in 1942, was three times mentioned in dispatches during the Second World War, and for gallantry while serving in the Navy he was awarded the Distinguished Service Cross and Bar. In 1953 he was advanced to Commander of the Order of the British Empire, in 1973 he was knighted for services to nature conservation, and in 1987 he was appointed a Companion of Honour. He died of a heart attack in 1989, just before his eightieth birthday.

In recognition of her husband's achievements, Kathleen Scott was granted the style, dignity and precedence of the wife of a Knight Commander of the Most Honourable Order of the Bath. In 1922 Lady Scott married Edward Young, MP for Norwich, by whom, in 1923, she had a son, the writer Wayland Young. In 1927 Edward Young was made a Knight Grand Cross of the British Empire, and in 1935 he was raised to the peerage as Baron Kennet. He died in 1960, when Kathleen's son Wayland succeeded as the 2nd Lord Kennet. Kathleen Kennet, who continued to work professionally under the name of Scott, died from leukaemia in 1947, according to her elder son 'gay and carefree and magnificent until the very end'. She certainly retained her wit; she told James Lees-Milne the effort of keeping alive was killing her. Her statue of Captain Robert Falcon Scott stands in Waterloo Place, London.

Many of those who served under Captain Scott and survived went on to gain further distinction and honours:

Edward Atkinson (1882–1929), junior surgeon on the *Terra Nova*, was awarded the DSO at Gallipoli, was three times mentioned in dispatches, and in 1918 was awarded the Albert Medal for gallantry following an explosion in his ship HMS *Glatton*, in which he lost an eye.

Michael Barne (1877–1961), second lieutenant on *Discovery*, was mentioned in dispatches four times during the First World War and was awarded the DSO.

Louis Bernacchi (1876–1942), physicist aboard *Discovery*, was awarded the US Navy Cross in the First World War and was appointed to the military division of the OBE.

Victor Campbell (1875–1956), lieutenant on the *Terra Nova*, won the DSO in the Dardanelles.

Thomas Crean (1876–1938), an able seaman on *Discovery* and Petty Officer on *Terra Nova*, was awarded the Albert Medal for the heroic part he played in saving the life of Lieutenant Edward Evans when he was stricken with scurvy.

Frederick Dailey (b.1873), a carpenter on *Discovery*, was mentioned in dispatches during the First World War, was commissioned at sea and awarded the DSC.

Edward Evans (1881–1957), lieutenant on the *Terra Nova*, won the DSO and too many foreign decorations and honours to list, became a rear admiral, and in 1945 was created Lord Mountevans.

Tryggve Gran (1889–1980), ski instructor with the *Terra Nova*, served as a captain in the Royal Flying Corps and was mentioned in dispatches. By 1977 he had become the sole survivor of the *Terra Nova* expedition. He died near Oslo at the age of ninety.

William Lashly (1868–1940), leading stoker on *Discovery*, was, like Thomas Crean, awarded the Albert Medal for saving the life of Lieutenant Evans. He asked to be buried with no headstone on his grave.

Raymond Priestley (1886–1972), geologist aboard *Terra Nova*, became vice-chancellor of Melbourne University and president of the Royal Geographical Society. He was knighted in 1949.

Charles Royds (1876–1931), lieutenant with *Discovery*, became assistant commissioner of the Metropolitan Police, was appointed vice admiral and KBE, and dropped dead in 1931 while dancing at a charity ball at the Savoy.

George Simpson (1878–1965), meteorologist on *Terra Nova*, became director of the Meteorological Office in London and was knighted in 1938.

Reginald Skelton (1872–1956), lieutenant with *Discovery*, was awarded the DSO after the Battle of Jutland. He became a vice admiral and was created KCB.

N O T E S

Chapter One

1. Vice Admiral Harry Cuming (1832–96).

2. Scott's entry in the *Dictionary of National Biography* is currently incorrect in a number of particulars. It states that he was the second son, passed into HMS *Britannia* in 1880, became a midshipman in 1882, and was promoted lieutenant in 1897. His entry in *Who Was Who* also has his entry into HMS *Britannia* wrong. Many details previously published about Scott's naval career need to be treated with caution. All dates and postings quoted here are taken from official naval records held at Dartmouth and Greenwich.

3. In 1964 the school moved to Ascot, and unfortunately no archive material prior to that date has been preserved.

4. This and the following quotations are from Scott's conduct sheet in *Britannia*, Royal Naval Archives, Greenwich.

5. Elspeth Huxley, *Scott of the Antarctic* (1977). Hereafter Huxley, *Scott*.

6. Harry Ludlam, *Captain Scott: The Full Story*. Hereafter Ludlam, *Scott*.

7. Knighted in 1912, and in 1944 raised to the peerage as Baron Courtauld-Thomson.

8. Huxley, *Scott*.

9. Huxley, *Scott*.

10. Huxley, *Scott*.

11. In 1897 Ettie married the 45-year-old MP for South Antrim and Parliamentary Secretary to the Admiralty, William Ellison-Macartney, and there is a strange story that in 1898, when Scott was at his sister's house in Walton Street to enquire about the progress of her first confinement, he fainted on the

doorstep from anxiety. Ettie's marriage was socially very prestigious. Her husband had been educated at Eton and Exeter College, Oxford, where he took a BA with first class honours. In 1900 he was made a Privy Councillor, and eight years later he served as High Sheriff for County Antrim. He became Governor of Tasmania and then of Western Australia, and in 1918 he was appointed KCMG.

Rose married Eric Campbell of the Royal Irish Fusiliers, who died in 1906. Kate married Harry Brownlow, a surgeon from Henley-on-Thames.

12. Huxley, *Scott*.
13. An explanation of the magnetic Poles has been furnished by Huxley in *Scott*, which surely cannot be improved upon, and is here reproduced by kind permission of Mrs Huxley, who sadly died while this book was in preparation. She wrote:

> A brief explanation of the magnetic Poles in simple non-scientific terms seems virtually impossible to formulate, beyond saying that they are the spots on earth's surface, one in the Arctic and one in the Antarctic regions, where the end of a freely suspended compass needle will point straight down. The major source of earth's magnetic field stems from an electrical current system within the core of earth itself, but owing to little-understood variations in this system, magnetic poles move about. The current South magnetic Pole [Mrs Huxley was writing in 1977] is in the coastal region of George V Land, but in a few years' time it will have moved on. Variations in the field have a connection with sunspots. Much still remains to be discovered about this very complex system.

CHAPTER TWO

1. Later First Sea Lord and 1st Marquess of Milford Haven (1854–1921). His wife lived until 1950.
2. Robert Falcon Scott, *The Voyage of the 'Discovery'* (1905). Hereafter Scott, *Voyage*.
3. Huxley, *Scott*.

4. Ludlam, *Scott*.
5. Huxley, *Scott*.
6. Albert Armitage, *Two Years in the Antarctic* (1905).
7. Huxley, *Scott*.
8. One of Shackleton's sons, Edward, was destined to enjoy a distinguished career, receiving a life peerage in 1958 and the Order of the Garter in 1974.
9. Instructions given to Scott by the Royal Geographical Society.
10. Scott, *Voyage*.
11. Ludlam, *Scott*.
12. Scott, *Voyage*.
13. Scott, *Voyage*.
14. Scott, *Voyage*.
15. Louis Bernacchi, *The Saga of the Discovery* (Blackie & Sons, 1938).
16. Scott, *Voyage*.
17. Scott, *Voyage*.

CHAPTER THREE

1. Ludlam, *Scott*.
2. Scott, *Voyage*. The next quotations are from the same source.
3. Ludlam, *Scott*.
4. Scott, *Voyage*.
5. Ludlam, *Scott*.
6. Ludlam, *Scott*.
7. Ludlam, *Scott*.
8. Scott's promotion to CVO was gazetted on 11 October 1904.
9. Not No. 22 Eccleston Square, Huxley, *Scott*.
10. Roland Huntford, *Scott and Amundsen* (1979). Hereafter Huntford, *Scott*.
11. In addition, Scott was presented with medals from Holland, Denmark and Sweden, and was given honorary membership of the Russian Geographical Society.
12. Ludlam, *Scott*.
13. Scott was also a member of the Marlborough Club. This was not his first experience of an accident at sea. In 1893 he ran a torpedo boat aground in Falmouth harbour.

14. Huxley, *Scott*.
15. Elspeth Huxley, *Peter Scott: Painter and Naturalist* (1993).
16. James Lees-Milne, *Ancestral Voices* (1975). Lees-Milne has also provided an essay on Kathleen Scott, titled 'Kathleen Scott', in *Fourteen Friends* (1996). See also a biography of Kathleen Scott by her granddaughter Louisa Young, *A Great Task of Happiness: The Life of Kathleen Scott* (1995).
17. Zoë Thomson's husband has previously been mistakenly identified as Archbishop of Canterbury.
18. Huxley, *Scott*, is in error in saying that Scott wore naval uniform.
19. Not Kathleen's brother Rosslyn, who did not even sign the register (Young, *A Great Task of Happiness*).
20. Ludlam, *Scott*.
21. A snide suggestion by Roland Huntford (in *Scott*) that Scott had to be 'summoned to London at the proper time in [Kathleen's] menstrual cycle' seems quite unjustified.
22. Huxley, *Scott*.
23. 6,000 volunteers is the number related by Scott's widow to Lees-Milne *(Ancestral Voices)*. Some people have put the figure higher.
24. Lees-Milne, *Ancestral Voices*.
25. Huxley, *Scott*.

CHAPTER FOUR

1. Huntford, *Scott*.
2. Huxley, *Scott*.
3. Huntford, *Scott*.
4. Robert Falcon Scott, *Scott's Last Expedition* (1913). Hereafter Scott, *Expedition*.
5. Scott, *Expedition*.
6. Huxley, *Scott*.
7. Scott, *Expedition*.
8. Scott, *Expedition*.
9. Scott, *Expedition*. The following quotations are from the same source.
10. The word 'ski' is Norwegian and the plural 's' was never used until the word became anglicized.

11. Some of the nicknames acquired by members of the second expedition were rather odd. Lieutenant Harry Pennell was known as Penelope, and the parasitologist, Edward Atkinson, as Jane. Scott himself was called the Owner, naval slang for the captain of a warship.
12. Scott, *Expedition*. The remaining quotations in the chapter are from the same source.

CHAPTER FIVE

1. Scott, *Expedition*.
2. Huxley, *Scott*.
3. James Lees-Milne, *Prophesying Peace* (1977).
4. Huxley, *Scott*.
5. Scott, *Expedition*.
6. Apsley Cherry-Garrard, *The World Journey in the World* (1922). A vivid account of the episode, based on this book and called, perhaps ironically, 'A Bad Time', was written by Nancy Mitford and appeared in a collection of her essays, *The Water Beetle* (1962).
7. Scott, *Expedition*.
8. Huxley, *Scott*.
9. Huxley, *Scott*.
10. Scott, *Expedition*.
11. Huxley, *Scott*.
12. Huxley, *Scott*.
13. Huxley, *Scott*.
14. Huxley, *Scott*.
15. Huxley, *Scott*.
16. Huxley, *Scott*.
17. Scott, *Expedition*.
18. Matthew Parris, *Scorn: With Added Vitriol* (1994).
19. Scott, *Expedition*.
20. Scott, *Expedition*.

CHAPTER SIX

1. All quotations in this chapter are taken from Scott, *Expedition*.

SELECT
BIBLIOGRAPHY

Armitage, Albert. *Two Years in the Antarctic*, Arnold, 1905

Bernacchi, Louis. *The Saga of the 'Discovery'*, Blackie & Sons, 1938

Brent, Peter. *Captain Scott and the Antarctic Tragedy*, Weidenfeld & Nicolson, 1974

Cherry-Garrard, Apsley. *The Worst Journey in the World*, Constable, 1922

Evans, Edward Ratcliffe G.R. *South With Scott*, Collins, 1921

Gwynn, Stephen. *Captain Scott*, John Lane, 1929

Hattersley-Smith, Geoffrey (ed.). *The Norwegian with Scott* (The diaries of Tryggve Gran, translated by his daughter, Ellen McGhie), National Maritime Museum, 1984

Huntford, Roland. *Scott and Amundsen,* Hodder & Stoughton, 1979

Huxley, Elspeth. *Peter Scott: Painter and Naturalist*, Faber & Faber, 1993

———. *Scott of the Antarctic*, Weidenfeld & Nicolson, 1977

King, Harold G.R. (ed.). *Diary of the 'Terra Nova' Expedition to the Antarctic 1910–1912*, Blandford Press, 1971

Lashly, William. *Under Scott's Command*, ed. A.R. Ellis, Gollancz, 1969

Select Bibliography

Lees-Milne, James. *Ancestral Voices*, Faber & Faber, 1975

———. *Prophesying Peace*, Chatto & Windus, 1977

Ludlam, Harry. *Captain Scott: The Full Story*, W. Foulsham, 1965

Mitford, Nancy. *The Water Beetle*, Hamish Hamilton, 1962

Pound, Reginald. *Scott of the Antarctic*, Cassell, 1966

Savours, Ann (ed.). *Scott's Last Voyage Through the Antarctic Camera of H. Ponting*, Sidgwick & Jackson, 1974

Scott, Robert Falcon. *The Voyage of the 'Discovery'*, Smith, Elder, 1905

———. *Scott's Last Expedition*, Smith, Elder, 1913

Seaver, George. *Scott of the Antarctic*, John Murray, 1940

Wilson, Edward A. *Diary of the 'Discovery' Expedition to the Antarctic 1901–1904*, ed. Ann Savours, Blandford Press, 1966

Young, Louisa. *A Great Task of Happiness: The Life of Kathleen Scott*, Macmillan, 1995

POCKET BIOGRAPHIES

This series looks at the lives of those who have played a significant part in our history – from musicians to explorers, from scientists to entertainers, from writers to philosophers, from politicians to monarchs throughout the world. Concise and highly readable, with black and white plates, chronology and bibliography, these books will appeal to students and general readers alike.

Available

Beethoven
Anne Pimlott Baker

Mao Zedong
Delia Davin

Alexander the Great
E.E. Rice

Sigmund Freud
Stephen Wilson

Marilyn Monroe
Sheridan Morley and
Ruth Leon

Rasputin
Harold Shukman

Jane Austen
Helen Lefroy

POCKET BIOGRAPHIES

Forthcoming

Marie and Pierre Curie
John Senior

Ellen Terry
Moira Shearer

David Livingstone
Christine Nicholls

Margot Fonteyn
Alistair Macauley

Winston Churchill
Robert Blake

Abraham Lincoln
H.G. Pitt

Charles Dickens
Catherine Peters

Enid Blyton
George Greenfield